HOME FELLOWSHIP MEETINGS

HOME FELLOWSHIP MEETINGS

By
Bill Scheidler

Bible Temple Publications
Portland, Oregon

Available from:
Bible Temple Publications
7545 N.E. Glisan St.
Portland, Oregon 97213
U.S.A.

ISBN 0-914936-14-X
PRINTED IN U.S.A.

TABLE OF CONTENTS

CHAPTER ONE

The Problem

It is clear that the church is approaching a great day of visitation and out-pouring. Everywhere you go today in Christendom there is a feeling that the second coming of Christ is approaching. People are talking everywhere about the prophetic time-table of God and it is not uncommon to hear Christians greet one another with the phrase "Jesus is coming soon!" More and more preachers are beginning to declare "I believe we are the last generation".

Certainly, this situation is not unique to this century of believers. Even the disciples in the early church had a sense of imminency with regard to the return of the Lord. Indeed every major revival since the apostolic period has been marked by a similar expectation. In fact, a careful examination will show that the most unproductive periods of church history were when believers had no such expectation.

So why should we feel that this generation is any different? Why should we presume that we are on the crest of the endtime? For the simple reason that never before in the history of the church have so many specific prophecies been fulfilled, and has the world been in such a strategic position for the remainder of endtime prophecy to be fulfilled. The signs of the times are all around us and it is not just a small segment of Christendom that is observing these signs.

Many books on the market today are filled with insight on this generation. Unfortunately, many books speak only of the negative aspects of the day of the Lord. They speak of wars and famine, they speak of backsliding and apostacy, they speak of natural calamities, persecution and distress. While all of these negative things are indeed predicted by Christ there is also a positive side to Christ's predictions concerning the end times.

It is clear in the Bible that while the love of many will wax cold and many will fall away yet, the endtime will also be marked by the greatest harvest and ingathering of souls that the world has ever seen (Matthew 13:27-30,39). In addition to a numerical expansion in the kingdom of God, the end times will be marked by a church that has come to full stature (Ephesians 4:13-16), is without spot and wrinkle (Ephesians 5:25-27) and is a sharp threshing instrument moving mightily against Satan and the kingdom of darkness (Romans 16:20).

In other words the end time will be marked by great visitation and revival where multitudes will be swept into the church. Christ's parable of the kingdom, Peter's miracle drought of fish, and Joel's vision of the latter rain outpouring, all seem to indicate that the "glory of the latter house" will far surpass anything that has been seen heretofore.

What does all this mean for the church? What does this mean for pastors in the end time? It surely means many things, but one thing is obvious, many people are going to be saved in the churches, which means many fish are going to have to be cleaned.

Multitudes of people have always brought with them multitudes of problems. In Acts 6 when the number of the disciples was multiplied suddenly problems, murmurings and greater needs arose. What is the church to do? What is the pastor to do? How can the church minister effectively to the needs of people? Can one man standing behind the "sacred desk" one hour per week effectively meet the need? How does one man touch the lives of 1000, 2000 or 10,000 people? How can a church handle the very thing for which it has prayed for centuries — growth?

Many churches in America today have begun to grow rapidly. As they have, they have crossed a line where they have had to make a choice in their ministry. When the church gets large, five changes can easily take place.

1. The church becomes *program oriented* rather than *people oriented.* All the energy of the pastoral staff must be given to keeping programs going that will hopefully touch people's lives. Soon people can get the feeling that programs are more important than people and that they are only a small part of a massive, insensitive piece of equipment.

2. The church becomes guilty of *pulpit pastoring* rather than *personal pastoring.* The pastor preaches a shot gun message on Sunday morning hoping to hit the needs of most of the people, but never able to minister to the personal needs of any one person. The individual has no personal relationship to his pastor and the pastor cannot even call his own sheep by name.

HOME FELLOWSHIP MEETINGS

3. The church becomes an *assembly hall* rather than an *assembly line*. The church is to be a place where people's lives are put together and where that which is missing is put into place. In many large churches, however, it is easy to feel that church attendance is the only important barometer of spiritual life and that the only value an individual has is to fill a certain spot once a week. As long as he is "not forsaking the assembling" together he is doing fine.

4. The church becomes *an orphanage* rather than a *family*. It is difficult to raise children effectively in a group. One or two parents for 50 children will never be able to develop an intimate relationship and fellowship with those children. Most likely the children themselves will never feel close to one another.

5. The church becomes *a ministry center* rather than *a ministry factory*. When a church becomes so large it is difficult to help each person enter into their own ministry. We can only offer certain services to people that will hopefully keep them going for another week rather than effectively equipping the saints for the work of ministering.

God is placing a great challenge before the church in these days, it is the challenge for growth. It is fairly easy to assist a group of 25 people to become mature men and women of God, but how can one man handle a multitude? God wants large churches. He created the church for growth. All the principles of God's Word must be workable for small churches and large churches alike. God is raising up an army of trained servants in these days to march effectively against the gates of hell. There must be a way to fulfill His glorious commission.

CHAPTER TWO

The Solution

The problem facing the church today is not unlike the problem faced by Moses when he led the people of God out of Egypt and toward the land of promise. Here was one man trying to be the chief counselor and decision maker for all 3,000,000 people. It sounds absolutely ridiculous when you think about it and yet, sometimes you can be so close to a problem that you cannot see the obvious solution. It took a visit from his father-in-law to pin-point a serious problem.

The problem in Israel was serious for a couple of reasons. First of all, Jethro was careful to point out that Moses was going to wear away (Exodus 18:23). When a pastor is ministering to a small number of people, he can do it all, and usually does. But as the number of people increases he must begin to release responsibility to others or the burden will become heavier and heavier for him to bear.

When Jethro came to visit his daughter he had no time to spend with Moses, because Moses was never home. When you pastor 3,000,000 people there is always someone in trouble or going through a difficult problem. Moses loved the people more than his own life. Therefore he put his own personal needs after their needs. This left Moses with no time for himself, his family or his personal relationship to God. When you love people and you have a desire to help them this is usually the result.

Every morning when Moses got up there was a line outside his tent; people who needed answers; people whose lives were in turmoil; people who had to make critical decisions about their life and future. How could Moses say no to these people? He didn't! Every day from sun up to sun down Moses talked, shared, and counseled with people. Day after day, week after week, month after month, it was the same. The waiting line never went away and Moses was wearing away.

Jethro did not need a special revelation to know that Moses would never last at this pace. Out of concern for Moses and his own

6

THE SOLUTION

daughter, he had to rebuke Moses to spare his life. No one man was ever meant to carry the burden of so many people. "The thing you are doing is not good" (Exodus 18:17).

In addition to Moses' health, there was another reason that the situation was serious. Jethro saw that what was taking place was not good for the people. People just cannot stand in line day after day without getting frustrated. If people know that you are too busy, they will wait until the problems are so big that only a "wizard" will be able to solve them. In addition, if people have to wait so long in line they will be tempted to not come at all, or give up before they see the leader.

Jethro saw that as long as Moses was by himself and continued his present approach to things, the job would not get done and the people's needs could not be met. If this condition was to continue it would surely jeopardize the entire plan of God to bring a believing people into the promised land.

Jethro then proceeded to give Moses some fatherly advice which later proved to be the same advice that God gave to Moses (Numbers 11, Deuteronomy 1). He suggested two main changes in Moses' approach.

First, he suggested that Moses take up the mantle of teaching on a corporate basis. Rather than individually trying to teach each person divine principles as they were going through problems, he suggested that Moses begin to publicly teach all of the people in three main areas and in doing so he would equip them to make many of their own decisions, because they would have truth to draw upon. He told Moses to teach the people the word, the way and the work. That is, he should teach them the word of God including the principles, commands and precepts. He should teach them how to walk in the ways of God. And he should teach them their personal responsibility before the Lord.

By doing this the people would have the resources to take care of most of their own problems. Many problems that people have are really basic, and are similar in nature. The same principles can apply to many different situations. Moses as the chief shepherd in Israel needed to let his voice be heard in corporate teaching and instruction.

The second suggestion that Jethro made was that Moses bring

others into his job. He encouraged Moses to select qualified men from among God's people who had their lives in order, and to delegate some of his reponsibility to them. He gave him the old method of "divide and conquer". Jethro suggested that he place these men over groups of people to hear their cases and he should only be involved in the matters that were too difficult for these appointed representatives. Moses saw the wisdom of this advice and added many years to his life as a result.

In the New Testament we see a similar thing taking place early in the life of the Church. Because the heart of the leadership was that of servants, it became very easy for the leaders to be personally involved with every need in the church. When the number of the disciples multiplied this became an ever increasing impossibility. As a result, the needs of some were neglected (Acts 6:1-6). An even worse thing took place, however, because the apostles found that in order to meet all the pressing practical needs of the body, they had to reduce their personal time in prayer and the word. As a result their public ministry was hindered.

They too learned very quickly that "many hands make light work". They chose other able men to share in the task of ministering to the personal needs of the growing Church. As a result the needs of the people were met and the word of God increased in power (Acts 6:7).

Today the Church is facing the same challenge of growth. It is exciting to see the promises of harvest coming to pass. However, as the people come they will come with great needs. The Church must be prepared in advance to minister effectively to these needs. The solution that Moses found and the solution discovered by the early apostles still works today. That solution could be summarized as follows:

1. Concentrate in public on the preaching and teaching of the word, focusing on principles of practical Christian living.
2. Divide the congregation into segments as Jesus did when He fed the 5,000 (Luke 9:14; John 6:10-11).
3. Place over these segments men who are qualified to bear such responsibility.
4. Work to train and equip these men to feed on their level.

CHAPTER THREE

The Purpose for Homemeetings

The New Testament Church had a two-pronged plan of attack in ministering to the needs of people. They had the public gathering, which was absolutely vital for the worship life, inspiration and marching orders for the church. They also had a smaller gathering. They continued in the temple *and* in every house teaching and preaching (Acts 5:42). Paul preached publicly *and* from house to house (Acts 20:20). The public gathering is important for the unity of the Church and outreach potential. The smaller gathering is important for many other reasons.

There are many purposes for having homemeetings. Homemeetings are not meant to be in competition with the corporate gathering. On the contrary the homemeeting should be a tremendous compliment to the corporate assembly life. The homemeeting will succeed only on this level. If the homemeeting is competing with the main Church gathering it will become divisive, repetitious and perhaps even boring. But, if the homemeeting meets needs that are not being touched in any other phase of body life they will be full of life.

At Bible Temple we have three main opportunities for corporate involvement. Each opportunity meets different but equally important needs among God's people (see chart on page XX). The Sunday services focus on corporate worship and hearing a present word and challenge from the Lord. The mid-week service focuses on the systematic teaching of the Word of God. The homemeeting involves a giving of ourselves to one another in the body of Christ. All of these are important. None of these are in competition with each other.

THE PURPOSE FOR HOMEMEETINGS

BIBLE TEMPLE SERVICES		
CORPORATE MEETINGS		**HOME-MEETINGS**
Truth Opportunity Provided	Truth Opportunity Provided	Relationships Opportunity Provided
SUNDAY SERVICES	* THURSDAY "ACTION" NIGHT	TUESDAY, NIGHT HOMEMEETINGS
Giving ourselves to the Lord corporately	Giving ourselves to the Word systematically	Giving ourselves to the body personally
• Preaching Emphasis Truth bringing decisions • Corporate worship in Spirit and in truth	• Teaching Emphasis Truth bringing understanding • Biblical, doctrinal, and practical instruction	• Fellowship Relationships bringing involvement and interpersonal growth • Body ministry

In every Church the homemeeting may take on a different emphasis depending on the vision of the local church. Because of my personal involvement with Bible Temple in Portland, Oregon, much of the remainder of this book will be a reflection of what we have done and why we have done it. Perhaps our experience and the sharing of it will help other pastors and churches to enhance the experiences of the members of their respective churches.

There are at least seven purposes that the homemeeting can serve in a congregation. Each one of them has some validity in and of itself. Depending on the vision of the church and the personality of the church, some will be emphasized more than others, but it is comforting that all seven purposes can be met at the same time through this expression.

1. A Deeper Level of Personal Ministry to the Needs of God's People.

As the congregation grows in size it is really impossible for a pastor or even a pastoral team to touch each person on a regular, consistent basis. There comes a time in the life of a church where it is even difficult to know the name of each person. Nothing can be more frustrating to a pastor who has a genuine heart to be personally involved

HOME FELLOWSHIP MEETINGS

in the lives of his people. Through the homemeeting each person can be ministered to on a regular basis by a trained leader in the church. Someone who loves them and knows where they are in relation to the Lord. When they are hurting, someone knows about it. When they are rejoicing, others are rejoicing with them. When they have a need, the need will be seen and served. The rest and peace of mind that this can bring to a pastor is tremendous.

2. A Greater Opportunity for Individual Ministry and Function in the Body.

We know that each member of the body of Christ has a ministry. When we come together there should be opportunities given for members of the body to express themselves (I Corinthians 14:26). However, in a large assembly it is not practical for each person to share a testimony, a scripture, a song, a prophecy, an exhortation, a prayer or a teaching. Unless the church service becomes a marathon meeting, only a few can share in each public gathering.

In a homemeeting, however, where there are only fifteen to twenty people present, it is not difficult for every person to make a contribution to the meeting. In this setting every member of the body has an opportunity for a ministry outlet. In the homemeeting, every believer can actively communicate their faith to others in the body.

3. A Deepening of the Level of Personal Relationships in the Body.

One of the complaints that is often leveled against a large church is that it is difficult to get to know people and feel like you belong to a family. Many feel like they are part of an organization or a machine rather than a church. It is difficult to fellowship with people if your only experience with them is viewing the back of their head once a week on Sunday morning. People in a large assembly can feel like "strangers" for many months.

The beautiful thing about the homemeeting is that it has the potential in a large church of preserving the family atmosphere. In the homemeeting every person can feel like they are a vital, needed part. They can get to know people eye to eye. They also can be well known and cared for by others. The homemeeting is a great place to develop intimate, interpersonal relationships with other people.

THE PURPOSE FOR HOMEMEETINGS

4. A Practical Way of Bringing New Members into the Life and Flow of the Body.

When a church is large people can get lost in the shuffle. In fact, if a person wants to, he can stay hidden for months. When you introduce yourself to someone and ask if they are a visitor and they reply, "I've been coming here for 5 years", then you know that this is possible. Many of these people are not really involved in the church in any way and represent a vast untapped resource of personnel for all kinds of activities in and around the church.

In a smaller setting it is easier to feel a part, easier to see where people's gifts and talents lie and easier to get people involved. When people are involved with each other, they have a greater sense of belonging. They sense they are needed and that they have something vital to contribute.

5. A Greater Sense of Responsibility for the Local Community.

In a large city it is difficult for people to feel a real burden for their own neighborhood because of the city's great size. However, as believers meet in their own neighborhoods they can begin to develop such a desire. This desire will find expression in a greater burden for neighborhood evangelism, a greater involvement in community affairs and a more active participation in local politics.

It has been amazing to see how few people realized just how close they lived to other members of the church. Many people had been virtual neighbors for years and did not realize it. As they met in the homemeeting, beautiful relationships were established between these people.

6. A More Effective Way to Raise Up and Establish Future Leaders in the Church.

In every church there are those who feel called by God to leadership ministries. Many churches have sought to train these leaders through education. Education is essential for all leaders and yet education in and of itself does not produce or prove leaders. Church leaders must have a thorough working knowledge of the Word of God but they must also have a servant's heart and a genuine love for people. You can equip and test leaders in the area of knowledge in the classroom, but there must be a practical involvement to test the heart of the leader.

HOME FELLOWSHIP MEETINGS

In the homemeeting setting, leaders can grow and develop under other more seasoned ministries. They are able to gradually work into more and more areas of responsibility as they grow and develop. They can put into practice all of the things that they are learning intellectually.

7. An Effective Alternative in the Event of an Emergency Situation.

It is not totally outside of the realm of possibilities that an occasion could arise where the corporate church would not be able to gather. An emergency could arise of a political, natural or economic nature, that could at least interrupt normal church activities. Such things have happened in other countries. Locally, we have had weather patterns that made extensive travel very difficult. In times of fuel shortages officials have considered limiting or even curtailing travel on Sundays.

Whatever the situation, the church should have the capability to carry on. If the church could not meet corporately for any reason, it could continue to meet through the homemeeting. What a blessing that the church's success is not tied to a particular set of natural benefits or circumstances.

All of these seven purposes are serviced through the homemeeting. Depending on the vision of each individual church, one or more of these purposes will be emphasized above the others. In addition, other purposes such as teaching, may be important to some. Whatever the case, it is plain that the opportunity for enrichment to the body is unlimited.

CHAPTER FOUR

Structuring the Homemeeting

When it comes to structuring any program in the church there are usually several options from which to choose. Many churches today are using the homemeeting to enhance the program of the church and there are a variety of methods represented by them. Ultimately every church must decide what works best for them, but after many years of experience with the homemeeting it seems that some forms are better than others.

The structure of the homemeeting is important just as the structure of the human body is important. We do not make structure our focus, but ultimately our structure will enhance or hinder our overall purpose. If our purpose is going to be accomplished, our structure must correspond to it. Let us look at the various methods being used.

VARIOUS HOMEMEETING MODELS

1. The Leader Orientation

Many churches have used this approach with some success. They begin with a certain number of potential leaders. When the leader is approved, people are given the opportunity to choose the leader they want until a maximum number is reached. As greater needs arise, more leaders are added and growth is reflected in new home-meetings.

There are many potential problems with this model from the pastoral point of view. First of all, people can get discouraged if they do not get the leader that they wanted. If they do not get the leader that they wanted, they may not be as enthusiastically involved with another meeting or leader.

Second, there can develop a spirit of competition among leaders that opens the door for spiritual pride. Those with the large groups are elevated and others are made to feel inferior. A party spirit can easily develop where people boast in their leader.

A third problem in this kind of homemeeting is that it can easily

STRUCTURING THE HOMEMEETING

become a closed group. Without new people coming in continually, the focus easily shifts from ministry to the needs of others, to introspection. The group can become ingrown and "clickish".

A fourth concern in relation to a leader orientated program is that the older groups will eventually contain only those who have been involved for a long season, whereas the new home groups will consist primarily of those who are new in the church or new to the program. The potential is for all the mature to be in one group and all the immature to be the newer groups. In order for the needs of the immature to be met effectively, they must have good healthy relationships with those who are more mature.

Another problem with this model is that it usually lacks the hospitality and evangelistic vision of other forms. When a house is full to capacity, it is difficult to reach out and encourage others to be involved. It is easy for people to get very comfortable with their group. But, if the group is small and there is plenty of room to grow, people will be more motivated to include and draw in others.

A final problem with the leader orientation model is that this model has the most potential of all models to bring division to a church. The leader has an opportunity to establish a long term relationship with his people and may begin to view himself as their pastor. Because of the intimacy of the group, people may become more loyal to their homeleader than the leadership of the church and a splinter group can result. It would be a terrible thing if a program that was designed to strengthen and bless the church ended up dividing or fragmenting the church. No one who begins a home-meeting program ever expects such a thing to happen to them. But then, most couples who get married do not expect their marriage to end in divorce. Unfortunately, they do!

2. The Interest Orientation

In this model the homemeeting groups are centered around common interests and ministries. Homegroups can be established on many different themes. Some groups may focus on evangelism while others share common hobbies. Almost any kind of a group can be formed. Usually, this kind of group starts with a great amount of enthusiasm because it puts people of similar interests and values next to each other.

HOME FELLOWSHIP MEETINGS

These groups can be very exciting and undoubtedly minister to a common need for relationship and fellowship. Many churches have used this model with a great deal of success, and there is no question that there is potential for great blessing here.

The interest orientated group serves several of the needs listed in the previous chapter but it cannot minister to all of the needs. What church leaders need to decide is the purpose and goal for the home-meeting. The purpose and goal will dictate the form that the meeting takes.

If the purpose of the homemeeting is to be an extension of the pastoral ministry of the church, then the interest orientated group is not the best model. These groups tend to be focused on, "what I can receive" from the group, rather than, "what I can give" to others. They tend to attract people that are just like themselves in strengths and weaknesses, rather than bringing together the diversity of the body.

3. *The Geographical Orientation*

The geographical model is perhaps the best model as an arm of the pastoral ministry of the church. This model helps to keep all of the purposes of the homemeeting in balance. Mature are mixed with the immature; the young are mixed with the old and new leadership is constantly surfacing from within.

One of the great advantages of this model is the burden for the community that is created. Because all of the members of the meeting live near each other, they have common concerns and can get involved together in seeing them met.

Another great advantage is the clear lines of responsibility that can be drawn. When divisions are made geographically, it can take the emotion out of an otherwise delicate decision.

On the basis of our experience, we would highly recommend the geographical approach to home fellowship meeting. In order to facilitate structuring the homemeeting, follow these simple steps:

1. Obtain the name and address of everyone who considers themselves to be part of your local church. This information could be obtained on a Sunday morning service by asking the congregation to fill out a form and drop it in the offering (See appendix).

STRUCTURING THE HOMEMEETING

2. Procure a large map of your community and pinpoint every family unit presently attending.

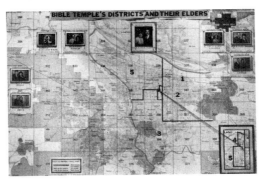

3. Divide this map into pastoral districts attempting to put an equal number of people into each district. The number of districts that you decide upon will be determined on the basis of the number of elders available to oversee such a district. You may also want to make the districts closer to the church smaller at first, because they will tend to grow more rapidly.
4. Divide each of the districts into zones. The number of zones will depend upon the number of people in each district. A good size to begin with is 20, because you really have no idea how many will actually attend the home-meeting at this time.
5. Appoint an elder over each district and a homeleader over each zone.
When making all divisions, care should be taken to use main arteries and through streets as much as possible. These make for natural boundaries and will be easier for all. In larger communities you may want to consider precinct lines so that homemeetings can also have more of a political voice.
Some adjustment may have to be made in those initial divisions after the meetings actually begin, depending on how many people actually attend. However, avoid making hasty changes. Let the first approach to the problem be an attempt to get everyone involved by drawing them into the group.

HOME FELLOWSHIP MEETINGS

The following would comprise the homemeeting structure (only one district division is used here as exemplary):

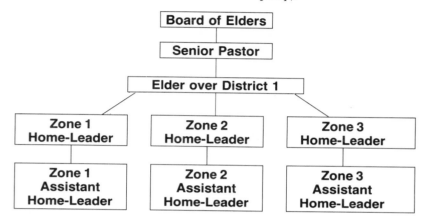

Each elder would have a district over which he has direct shepherding oversight. In small churches which have not yet adapted eldership, the senior pastor would fulfil this role. The district elder is responsible to the Board of Elders and to the Senior Pastor for the shepherding done in his district.

1. The elder of a district (or Senior Pastor) should never be a home-leader. Other promising ministries should be given this responsibility. It is the job of the elder to show, instruct, develop, and adjust his home-leaders so that they will become effective and productive shepherding ministries. It is not his duty to do it all himself.

2. The district elder should rotate between the homemeeting zones in his district. Thus he can observe the function of the home-leader and home meeting to evaluate its effectiveness. He also can offer his strength into the homemeeting he attends.

3. The district elder should meet regularly with his homemeeting zone leaders and their assistants. He should meet with them a minimum of once a month to discuss, advise, counsel, and correct any problems or procedures of the individual homemeetings. Because he is rotating the attendance of his homemeetings, he can notice weaknesses or areas which need improvement. He would

STRUCTURING THE HOMEMEETING

check on their shepherding of those with particular needs within the zones. He would also periodically devote a meeting to teaching how more effectively to do their job of shepherding others.

4. The district elder should keep a notebook of all those in his district. He would record here the names, addresses, zone meeting, monthly attendance, and any noteworthy problem areas of concern. This information he would obtain monthly from the zone home-leader.

5. The elder should himself report any serious problems to the senior pastor for counsel and to make him aware of the situation. When someone leaves the church, the district elder should try to visit the person(s). He should write a written report of the individual's cause for leaving. This is informative to the Senior Pastor and may be filed for future reference if ever needed.

CHAPTER FIVE

**Choosing a
Homeleader**

Choosing leaders in the house of the Lord is one of the greatest challenges and responsibilities given to pastors. In reality, this involves more of a recognition of leaders that God has placed in the body, than a choosing of leaders. Leaders must be shaped and molded by God through His special dealings and workings in their lives. The job of the pastor is to be able to recognize what God is doing in the lives of His people and make his placement of people in a way that is consistent with what God is saying and doing. To do this a pastor must not only be able to see and judge with the natural eye, but he must be able to discern what God is doing in the spiritual realm. This means that prayer and waiting on God should accompany any decision that the pastor may make.

The position of homeleader is a very important position in the body. It is a position of influence in the lives of God's people. As time progresses, this leader will have a profound influence on the lives of those to whom he has been ministering. Because of this, the selection of leadership is vital to the success of the homemeeting concept in a church and it should be a decision that involves the entire eldership of the church. Selection of leaders should be taken very seriously and should be a corporate decision of the church leadership. No one district pastor should take it upon himself to select the leader. Fortunately, God has given guidelines to the leadership that will aid in making a proper selection.

In Bible Temple, we have felt that the position of homeleader is such an important position, that no one should be placed in that position unless they qualify as deacons in the biblical sense. For this reason, we have actually made the position of the homeleader a deacon responsibility. A deacon is a servant to the body and an extension of the hands of the leadership. Each home leader is given the responsibility to care for seven to ten families, assisting the elders with their job of spiritual oversight over the people. The homeleader in reality serves as an assistant to the natural and spiritual needs of the people of God.

CHOOSING A HOMELEADER

Since we have identified the ministry of the homeleader as that of a deacon, we find great help when it comes to selecting homeleaders. God has given us very clear guidelines to use in the selection of deacons. He has given us a very detailed list of the kinds of qualities that a deacon must possess. As we evaluate possible candidates for the office of the deacon these qualifications must serve as the standard. If we ignore or disregard any of the qualifications that God has clearly laid out, we can be sure that we will have definite problems in the future. God's Word cannot be ignored if we want to prosper in any area of life and ministry.

The qualifications for the office of a deacon are summarized in Acts 6 and elaborated in detail in I Timothy 3. These qualifications are designed to protect God's people from the wrong kinds of leaders. God does not just want anyone ministering to His people. He is very concerned that His sheep get the best of care at the hands of those who are qualified to do so. He is not out looking for any and all volunteers. God expects deacons to have certain moral, domestic, spiritual and practical qualifications.

A. *Moral Qualifications*

The deacon must have a life that is exemplary to the people of God. He is a mature believer who has learned to control his tongue (I Timothy 3:8). A deacon must *not be double-tongued.* He is not a gossip. The homeleader will be in a position to know many things about many people, therefore, he cannot be the type of person who tells all. He must be very discreet concerning any private information he learns. This qualification also implies one who is loyal to those in leadership. Someone who is double-tongued is a person who says one thing to one person and gives a different view of it to another. A deacon must be loyal to the leadership in all of his conversation or he will become a sower of discord in the body.

The deacon must also be *blameless* (I Timothy 3:10). This means that in every area of life he must be above reproach. He is not involved in questionable things that will be a stumbling block to others. In other words, the deacon must be a mature (not perfect) believer, who has definitely made Christ and His kingdom first place in his life.

HOME FELLOWSHIP MEETINGS

The deacon must not be under the power of temporal things (I Timothy 3:8). Money, wine or other excesses cannot dominate his life. He is an overcomer who is disciplined in his personal walk and life.

Finally, the deacon must *be proven* (I Timothy 3:10). The word "proved" here means "to test, examine, scrutinize, to see whether a thing be genuine or not". For this reason a deacon should never be a new convert no matter how zealous he may be. New converts have not been tested in difficult situations as yet to see how they will stand. In addition, a deacon should not be someone who is new to the local body of believers. New people, no matter how talented and gifted, need an opportunity to prove their faithfulness and loyalty. People who join the church because they are offered a position will cause problems one day in the testing time.

B. Domestic Qualifications

The home and home life of the deacon is a very critical area. If the deacon does not have his own home in order, he cannot be an example to God's people. People will have little or no respect for a leader who cannot make the principles of God's Word work in his own home and his own marriage. A deacon must be *the husband of one wife* and he must *rule his own house well* (I Timothy 3:12).

Any ministry that a person has should be an expression of his life. Nothing demonstrates the fruit of a person's life more than his family and marriage. A person can often display a sense of spirituality to casual acquaintances but he cannot hide his true nature from his family. His family will be a reflection of him and his ministry.

C. Spiritual Qualifications

A deacon must be a spiritual person who has been *filled with the Holy Ghost and wisdom* (Acts 6:3). Natural ability is important, but there must be a dependence on the Spirit to minister spiritual life to people. He must be someone who lives faithfully according to the principles of truth found in God's Word (I Timothy 3:9). This person must be spiritually right with God so that along with material relief he might minister spiritual encouragement to the people of God.

CHOOSING A HOMELEADER

It is interesting how similar the qualifications of a deacon are to that of an elder. It appears that those who would use this position in the body well would be some of the best potential candidates for elders at a future time. Being a homemeeting leader would be another excellent way for a deacon to prove his ministry.

D. *Practical Qualifications*

In addition to the specific qualifications listed in I Timothy 3 and Acts 6 there are other admonitions concerning those who would be in leadership among God's people. These too, must serve as a standard for us to follow in establishing home fellowship leaders.

1. Leaders must be examples (I Timothy 4:12). An example is someone that can be followed as a true representative Christian. Leaders are to be examples in speech, behavior, love, spirit, faith and purity. The eyes of the people will be on those that are set in leadership.

2. Leaders must be faithful (II Timothy 2:2). A leader that is faithful is one that can be depended upon to follow-through on assignments. He is also one who is faithful to know where he should be, and when he should be there. This would include such things as church attendance, tithing, the prayer life of the church, punctuality and involvement.

3. Leaders must be in submission to authority (Hebrews 13:17). Every Christian is to be submitted to those in authority in their lives. The only thing that qualifies us to handle authority is by being submitted to authority. A man must be properly submitted to authority before he can be given greater authority (Matthew 8:8).

4. Leaders must have the necessary ability (I Peter 4:11). It is not enough to be a good Christian when it comes to leadership placement. All Christians are to be model Christians. A person must also have the ability to lead a group of people. He must have certain freedom in speaking and sharing. He must be personable and easy to approach. If the person is not gifted to lead in this way, the meeting will not be a success and people will eventually lose interest.

HOME FELLOWSHIP MEETINGS

5. Leaders must demonstrate *loyalty*. There is a danger in giving younger or less experienced men authority over people in that they can become disloyal and attempt to draw away people after themselves. No one should be made a homeleader whose loyalty has not been proven. However, this must not present a hesitancy to appoint those who have proven their loyalty over a period of time to the leadership and the House of the Lord. Sometimes disloyalty can develop over a period of time if certain attitudes are not adjusted and checked. Certain attitudes can develop through various stages until they manifest themselves in a spirit of disloyalty. If such attitudes were checked at an early stage, the problem may never have occurred.

Loyalty is the result of a submissive heart. It includes a team spirit (Phil. 1:27). It seeks to have one spirit and to move as one soul (Phil. 2:2, "one accord", i.e., "one soul"). It seeks a unity of one mind and one judgment (I Cor. 1:10). It seeks to flow together and to speak the same things as one voice (I Cor. 1:10).

One other area that is important in home leader selection is that the leadership of a home group should be seen as a team ministry. This is not to say that a mature single adult could not lead a homemeeting, but a married couple in this ministry should involve a husband and wife that flow well together. For this reason, both the husband and the wife should qualify and function together in all aspects of the homemeeting.

After seeing all these qualifications one wonders if anyone is suited to the ministry of a homeleader. The purpose of these qualifications is not to discourage us. It is to give us a goal. It is to give us something to strive for. Leaders do not have to be perfect, but leaders should be growing into the image of Christ. Leaders do not have to be sinless, but they should be steadily progressing toward the mark of the high calling in Christ Jesus. Leaders are to be those who are going the way before the people. Whenever leaders cease to grow personally, they lose their ability to inspire and direct God's people.

Pastors who are in the position of choosing leaders will be tempted often to lower the standard. It would be better to have fewer meetings with qualified leaders than many meetings with unqualified leaders.

CHOOSING A HOMELEADER

If you do not have enough leaders, be committed to raising some up. Reach out and through personal ministry, disciple some potential leaders and see what God will do.

A good way to raise up future homeleaders is to have an assistant homeleader in each meeting where it is possible. As they assist an experienced homeleader, they will be further equipped and trained for the same task. This makes it easy as the homemeeting grows, to divide the meeting when it is necessary. The leader can take half of the people and the assistant the other half. This way new leaders are always being trained and raised up. The same care should be exercised in choosing assistants as in choosing leaders.

At Bible Temple, we make the selection of leaders and assistants an entire eldership decision. The elder or pastor over the district involved will ask for the approval of a leader at a regular elders meeting. Prior to that meeting the pastor of the district will have submitted an evaluation form which indicates he has given serious attention to the qualifications of the person (The deacon evaluation form has been included in the appendix 3). The elders as a body make the final approval. This is an additional safeguard to the selection process.

God wants His people tended and cared for. God has chosen to do this through men and women that He has called. In response to God's calling those men and women must seek to qualify by bringing their lives under the leadership of Christ. As they do, God will lay more and more responsibility on them. The greatest charge that a man or woman can have is that of tending the flock of God. But with that responsibility, comes accountability. Therefore, we do not want to be careless in our selection of leaders. We want to be discerning, cautious and confident!

CHAPTER SIX

The Leader's Responsibility

It should be clear by now that the job of the homeleader is more than just leading a Bible study in a home a few times each month. The homeleader is not just attempting to fulfill a need in himself to be able to teach or preach. The homeleader is a vital link between the pastoral leadership and the people. The homeleader's ministry is an extension of the pastoral ministry in the church. The homeleader is not a pastor in the ordained sense of the word, but he is an assistant to the pastoral ministry of the church reaching into the lives of people.

Because of this integral relationship between the pastoral ministry of the church and the homeleader, the homeleader's responsibilities are closely tied to the responsibility of the pastor. As a deacon the homeleader must see himself as one who helps the pastoral oversight of the church to fulfill their God-given charge to the congregation. Just as the first seven deacons helped the early apostles in their responsibility to the widows, so the homeleader helps the elders (pastors) in their God-given charge to tend, watch over and care for the flock. Ultimately, the elders/pastors of the church are accountable before the Lord for this ministry. But in the deacons they have enlisted the support of others to help them to fulfill their charge.

It is important to keep this understanding at the forefront when defining the ministry and responsibility of the homeleader. The homeleader is not the pastor or shepherd over the people. He has been placed under the pastoral ministry to help that ministry do its job. Some homeleaders may eventually emerge as future pastors in the church, but as homeleaders they are to be faithful with that which is another man's (Luke 16:12). Because of this it is important that homeleaders not take undue initiative in the lives of the sheep without the knowledge of the pastor. They are not the ones that must give ultimate accountability for what takes place (Hebrews 13:7). The pastor must never be released from his sense of duty and

THE LEADER'S RESPONSIBILITY

responsibility toward the people just because he has appointed leaders among the people.

Having said all of this, however, there is also a need to have a clear understanding of the duties and responsibilities of a homeleader. When someone is given a charge or duty it is absolutely necessary that a job description go with that charge. If there are no clear guidelines for the position of the homeleader there will be a great deal of frustration among those who are attempting to function in this ministry. If you do not know what is expected of you it is difficult to know how well you are doing and if what you are doing is accomplishing the intended purpose.

The job description of a homeleader is vitally connected to the charge given to the pastoral ministry. This pastoral charge could be divided into four main areas. Pastors are shepherds who are set over the people of God to (1) seek and save that which was lost, (2) minister to the needs of the sheep, (3) assist the people in finding their place of ministry and function in the body, and (4) help people enter into deeper relationship with the Lord and other members of the body.

The task of the homeleader, then, is to help or assist the pastor in these four areas relative to the local assembly over which they have been placed. There are some very practical things that the home-leaders can do to assist the pastoral leadership in these areas.

A. To Seek and Save That Which Was Lost.

There are several ways in which the homeleader can help the pastoral leadership to fulfill this charge:
1. Watch carefully the church attendance of your people. It is difficult for a pastor over a large number of people to know how everyone is doing in this area of church attendance, but if you only have a small number of people to see it is not at all difficult. A homeleader should be able to spot his people and know how well they are doing. When people miss church the situation should be checked out. They may be sick or there may be other problems. In either case they probably need some encouragement. Not that our only goal in people's lives is church attendance, but church attendance often times is a barometer of people's spiritual health.

HOME FELLOWSHIP MEETINGS

2. Be on the look out for new people. In a large church it is difficult for the pastors to get in touch with all of the visitors and new people in the church. But by involving the homeleaders in this task, many people can be reached. When visitors come to the church the homeleader over their geographical area should make it his responsibility to reach out to them and get involved in their lives. Members of the church should make it a goal when meeting new people to introduce them to their homeleader as soon as possible.

3. Be available to and seek out those who are in need of counsel. The homeleader should help make the pastor aware of the spiritual needs of the people. The goal is to bring the saints to maturity. When the homeleader sees a need in the lives of the people, he should inform the elder or district pastor. If the pastor feels that the homeleader has the capability of following through, the homeleader should tend to it. Otherwise the pastor should follow through.

   This means that the homeleader should gradually begin to grow in his ability to counsel. Studying proven guidelines for counseling should be part of the homeleader's job description. Perhaps at times the pastor and homeleader can work together and in this kind of environment the leader can be further trained.

4. Emphasize community evangelism among the people. The homeleader should continually encourage the people to reach out to their neighbors and friends. He might even schedule activities together as a homemeeting that would focus on evangelism. As a homemeeting, they might have special nights that are designed to include non-christian friends and neighbors.

B. To Minister to the Needs of the Sheep.

People have many needs that cannot be met in a corporate meeting, and the homeleader can touch so many of these in such effective ways.

1. Call on the sick especially when hospitalized. Even Jesus recognized this as an important measure of practical love (Matthew 25:36-45). This is a special time of need when people need to be encouraged and lifted up. A daily contact should be made with them when they are in the hospital and regular contact (at least

every three days) should be made when they are not. Flowers and perhaps a card from the homemeeting at this time are especially meaningful.

2. Spend quality time in preparation for the meeting itself. The meeting itself is a great time to minister to needs. The homeleader should ask God for special direction. He should attempt to minister to the specific needs of the group. Through special prayer times great personal ministry can take place.

3. Encourage your people to minister to the practical needs of the group. There are often widows with special needs, a family out of work, someone having a baby, a couple getting married or a hardship case of one kind or another. All of these things are opportunities to get people actively involved in the lives of others.

   When these needs arise, seek to meet them as much as possible in the homemeeting group itself. Plan a baby shower, bridal shower, food shower or work day. When the needs are too big for the individual meeting, seek help from the district pastor and other home groups. The homemeeting should be a caring group.

4. Have special homemeeting projects to reach out in needy situations. As Christians, we are to do good to all men (Galatians 6:10). Perhaps there is a neighborhood situation that could use some attention; — a needy family on the block, a fire that destroyed a home, an elderly person who needs assistance. Make it a homemeeting project to reach out to these needs.

C. Assist People in Finding Their Place of Ministry and Function in the Body.

One of the primary objectives of leadership is to see people begin functioning in their particular place in the body of Christ. Often people need special encouragement and counsel to see this become a reality in their lives.

1. Aim at getting each person involved in the homemeeting itself. The homemeeting is a great proving ground for ministry. As the homeleader uses people in many areas, he is better able to see their abilities and capabilities to be used on a larger scale. There are many avenues of expression in the homemeeting in which people can be involved that will help measure their gifts. Some of

HOME FELLOWSHIP MEETINGS

these things include leading worship, singing special numbers, playing instruments, prophesying, sharing testimonies, organizing refreshments, baby showers, special retreats or activities, praying for the sick, working on special projects or even sharing a special teaching. As people excel in these areas they may be used in a broader way in district or corporate church activities.

2. Utilize the "Personal Inventory" in ministering to their needs. The "Personal Inventory" is a tool that we have found helpful in keeping the right kind of questions in the mind of the homeleader concerning the needs and ministries of the people. These sheets can be kept in a notebook and periodic entries made. An example of this sheet is included as an appendix (Appendix 4). The main questions included in the "Personal Inventory" are as follows and should be asked about each person in the homemeeting.

(1) What do I feel are their most pressing physical needs?
(2) What do I feel are their most pressing spiritual needs?
(3) What am I doing to help meet those needs?
(4) What do I feel is this person's function in the body of Christ?
(5) How am I helping this person to develop into their place of service?
(6) What factors are keeping this person from realizing their full potential in God?
(7) In what areas of ministry are they presently involved?
(8) Have they ever been ministered to by the prophetic ministry? If so, have you read their prophecy?
(9) Do they tithe regularly?
(10) Do they attend the following on a regular basis: Prayer service, Homemeeting, Action night, Sunday services?

Whether the "Personal Inventory" is used or not, these are the kinds of questions that every leader should be asking about each person in the homemeeting. The answers to these questions will help form the basis of the homeleader's personal ministry to his people.

3. Spend a regular time in prayer for each member of the homemeeting. Jesus prayed regularly for His disciples (Luke 22:32). He knew their weak points and their strong points. He prayed for their weaknesses to be strengthened, but He also prayed concerning the placement of each of them in the overall plan (Luke 6:12-13).

THE LEADER'S RESPONSIBILITY

As the homeleader spends a special time in prayer for each of his people, God will give him a divine burden and vision for that person. He will give him insight into the special needs of that individual and He will give him creative ideas concerning the involvement and ministry of that person. The leader will be able to rise from prayer with a new sense of dedication to, a new vision for, a greater love for and a new direction for the lives of his people. This is how Christ, Who is the Head, builds His church.

D. Help People Enter into Deeper Relationship with the Lord and Each Other.

The church is to be a family. It is to be a place of relationship. That relationship begins with a vertical relationship to the Lord. This becomes the foundation on which all other relationships must be built. The homeleader must be very concerned about cultivating in his people a good relationship to the Lord. The homemeeting needs to be more than a social club to provide intimate relationships between people. It must also be a place where people can grow in their relationship to God. This is why prayer, praise, worship, Bible study and singing should be integral parts of the homemeeting. There must be an upward focus.

However, there must also be a focus on horizontal, brother and sister relationships. A strong purpose for the homemeeting is to help cultivate inter-personal relationships in the body. The homemeeting should be a place where all of the ''one another'' admonitions in the scripture can be fulfilled. The Word of God admonishes us to:

> comfort one another (I Thessalonians 4:18),
> exhort one another (Hebrews 10:25),
> edify one another (Romans 14:19),
> admonish one another (Colossians 3:16),
> serve one another (I Peter 4:10),
> teach one another (Colossians 3:16),
> pray for one another (James 5:11),
> exercise compassion one for another (I Peter 3:8),
> bear one another's burdens (Galatians 6:2),
> be considerate one of another (Ephesians 4:32),
> use hospitality one to another (I Peter 4:9),
> fellowship one with another (I John 1:7).

HOME FELLOWSHIP MEETINGS

The homemeeting is to be a place where all of this takes place. Many of these things cannot take place in a large setting, but in a home group they must take place. The leader must do things that will facilitate getting the people involved in each others lives.

1. Encourage members of the group to have another family from the homemeeting over for an evening together. The homeleader should set the example of hospitality here by making it a goal to have every member of the homemeeting in his home once or twice a year. There is something about being in another person's home that binds people closer together and helps them get to know each other. The homeleader may even design activities that will encourage this. Progressive dinners can make it possible to be in everyone's home in one night. Rotating the location of the homemeeting to a different person's home on occasion would afford another opportunity.

2. Schedule several social-type activities. Homemeetings should not be a miniature church service. They should be relaxed, warm, open and informal. This does not mean that they will not have structure, but the structure should lend itself to personal relationships. It might be that every other meeting the emphasis could be on building relationships through social activities. There are recreational activities such as swimming, roller skating, volleyball, and putt-putt golf that promote group involvement. Most metropolitan areas also have scenic vistas, zoos and parks to visit. Special social activities that can take place in a home or backyard such as table games, christian video, and potlucks can be fun too. Many more activities are discussed in the chapter entitled "Homemeeting Activities". The goal of all of these is to spend time with each other in a relaxed environment so that close, warm relationships will build and grow. It takes time for relationships to grow.

3. Plan some special activities that go beyond the regular schedule. The more time that people can spend with each other, the better they get to know each other. The better that they get to know each other, the more likely they will be to reach out to each other in times of need. Some activities would be difficult to do on a homemeeting night, but they are things that have great potential

THE LEADER'S RESPONSIBILITY

in drawing people together including hiking trips, camp-outs, weekend retreats, men's breakfasts and ladies luncheons. These things should not be done too often so they do not interfere with the regular program of the church, but occasionally such activities can bring great blessing to those involved.

4. Get each member as involved as possible in the lives of the others. This can be done by praying for each in the meetings themselves. It can also happen as you encourage them to take each other's needs seriously. Having various members of the homemeeting share their testimony also will have the positive effect of making people feel more a part of the other members of the group. The closer the people become, the greater potential they have to become a caring community into which others can be drawn.

This is the basic job description of the homeleader. His goal is to assist the pastoral ministry of the church by helping him in these four main areas. In addition to what has been said, the leader will also be a great help if he turns in all homemeeting reports on time, notifies the pastor of any problems quickly, and stays in close communication with the district pastor at all times. When the home-leader is committed to these goals the overall purpose for the homemeeting will be realized.

CHAPTER SEVEN

The Host and the Home

The atmosphere and environment have a great effect on the final product. This is something that has been proven in many realms. If the atmosphere is pleasant and conducive to growth, positive things take place. If the atmosphere is poor and detrimental to growth then the results are negative. The same holds true of the homemeeting.

It is interesting in Christendom that there is so much emphasis on buildings and forms. At times we can certainly over emphasize these things. But to the degree that buildings and forms enhance the worship life of God's people, they are a needed emphasis. In an unpleasant environment it may be difficult to focus on God. Or in a luxurious environment it might be just as difficult. The structure or building should enhance the purpose for which it was intended.

All of this applies directly to the homemeeting and selecting the home and the hosts for such a meeting. The home and the hosts help to set the atmosphere and environment for the meeting perhaps more than anything else. If the atmosphere of the home is not conducive to health, life, growth and orderliness, then it will have a negative effect on the overall results. If the hosts of that home are not warm, cordial, open and loving then the atmosphere will be tense and strained.

A. Choosing the Home.

The home in which the meeting is held will either contribute or detract from the overall purpose for the homemeeting. Several aspects should be taken into consideration when choosing the home.
1. Size.
   A cramped homemeeting is doomed to fail. People must not feel uncomfortable in the home or they will begin to make excuses not to come. Many homes are simply not large enough to have a homemeeting. Look for a home that has a large front room, a large

finished basement or a living-dining room combination where chairs can be set in a circle and everyone can be seen. It should be large enough so that at least all of the adults are able to be seated on chairs. Children can often sit on the floor near their parents.

2. Location.

It is ideal, particularly in the larger geographical locations, that the homemeeting meet in a home that is as close to the geographical center of the zone as possible. This is not always possible because of other considerations that are perhaps more important, but if there is a choice, a central location is always the best.

3. Order.

When dealing with orderliness there are two extremes equally devastating to the homemeeting. On the one hand, you have the home that is chaotic. The chaos might be due to unruly children, an unkept home, or filth. All of these conditions will turn people away from the homemeeting. People will not be able to put their minds on the Lord in that kind of environment.

On the other hand, a home that is too neat and too clean can be just as detrimental. In some homes the hosts might be so fussy that no one can relax. The atmosphere is tense the whole time for fear a crumb will be dropped or a drink will be spilled. People will be on pins and needles the whole meeting. They can get their eyes so focused on their surroundings it can become a stumbling block to them.

The balance between these two extremes is the best, a comfortable, well-kept, open and orderly home.

B. Choosing the Host.

Hosts for the meeting should be gracious, warm, open and hospitable people who really want to have the meeting in their home. It is best that the homeleader not serve as the host for the meeting so that the responsibilities can be divided and the homeleader can help protect the hosts from possible inconsiderateness among the people. In addition, when the meeting is over it is easier for the homeleader to encourage people to leave promptly if it is not his home.

The hosts should be a married couple who have been in the church for a long enough season to be one with the leadership in heart and vision. Even though they will not necessarily be considered leaders

HOME FELLOWSHIP MEETINGS

in the church, the very fact that they have a meeting in their home gives them a certain amount of credibility among the people.

The hosts should be mature believers who demonstrate unity in their marriage . Nothing disturbs the atmosphere of a meeting any more than a married couple who are supposed to be ministering to people yet they themselves are not flowing together.

The hosts should be people who have their children in order. It may be that an older couple is hosting the meeting and this is not a factor, but if there are children involved it is important that they be well-mannered. Because it is their home, their children will be leaders among the children who attend the meeting.

The hosts should be people who have a spiritual value system. If they have a material value system, the slightest scratch on their furniture will send them "through the ceiling". When you regularly have many people in your home, things will occasionally get bumped, dropped or broken. Hopefully it will be rare, but if the hosts are not willing to accept this, it would probably be better if they were not hosts.

The hosts should be outgoing and friendly. There may be times when the first people arrive that they are the only ones there to entertain the guests. They should have a warm, friendly personality that invites others in and puts them at ease.

The hosts should enjoy entertaining. If they do not enjoy this ministry, they will not be able to hide it and no one will enjoy themselves (Acts 16:16).

Finally, the hosts should be disciplined people. On the meeting night the home should be straightened up, the dinner dishes cleaned up and everyone dressed properly well in advance of the meeting. No one should "catch" them unawares.

C. Hosting Responsibilities.

Apart from providing the actual home for the meeting, the responsibilities of the hosts are minimal. This is why even busy people could be considered for this function.

1. Setting up/cleaning up — The setting up for the meeting should be completed at least one half hour before the scheduled time for the meeting. There will always be those who will come earlier than expected. Chairs should be arranged in such a way that there are

THE HOST AND THE HOME

no "bad seats". Everyone should at least be able to see the leader of the meeting clearly.

2. Greeting the people — The hosts should greet the people at the door, invite them in and make sure they can find a seat. If the weather is such that coats and umbrellas are needed, the host should help them care for these items.

3. Preparing the refreshments — The hosts are not necessarily the ones responsible for providing the refreshments, but they should help make sure they are prepared and served properly. This means that details like napkins, cups, utensils and table arrangements are all taken care of. It should be noted that as much of this should be done before the meeting as possible. It is not good if the host is out of much of the meeting taking care of these things.

The atmosphere of the home will make a big difference in the success of the homemeeting. It will either add a positive dimension or take away from the overall potential of the meeting. Care should be given to its selection and instruction should be given to those who would serve in this way. When handled properly the setting for the homemeeting will be an inspiration to all.

CHAPTER EIGHT

Ingredients of a Successful Homemeeting

Putting a homemeeting together is like baking a cake. There are many ingredients that go together to make it what it is. If you were to eat only the individual ingredients one at a time it might not satisfy the taste buds. However, when all the ingredients are put together in the right combination the result is very pleasing to the taste. Each ingredient has its own purpose for being in the recipe. It might be possible to leave certain ingredients out, but not without sacrificing something in the overall presentation of the cake.

There are many ingredients that make for a good homemeeting. Not all of them must occur in each meeting, but in the overall plan they should be common functions. If anyone is missing it will detract from the overall effectiveness of the homemeeting. Each ingredient contributes its own spice to the finished product.

A. Natural Home Atmosphere

The home setting is ideal for the accomplishment of the intended purpose. The home setting is warm, relaxed, cheerful, intimate and non-threatening. It is really the best setting for this kind of ministry to take place. It is better than a room in the church, a restaurant or some other multi-purpose facility. There is some thing about this environment that helps people to relax, open up, lower their defenses and share intimately.

B. Singing, Praise and Worship

Singing has a unique ability to draw people together. It is not unlike a holiday family gathering where people gather round the piano and sing joyfully. People's hearts are united and centered on the things of the Lord in this atmosphere. The singing should not be as formal as a Sunday service. It should be relaxed and casual. Those who play musical instruments should be encouraged to bring them and use

INGREDIENTS OF A SUCCESSFUL HOMEMEETING

them during this time. Even children can be encouraged to play an active role here.

Worship is always a primary purpose for gathering together. We worship the Lord in our songs, our praise and yielding to the Spirit in humble adoration. This is always an appropriate way to begin a meeting whether it be a social activity night or a Bible study. Not only does worship create an atmosphere for God to speak and ministry gifts to flow, but it also gets everyone's spirit in tune with God's spirit.

C. Sensitivity to the Holy Spirit

Many times God wants to intervene in a special way in the homemeeting to minister to a unique need, bless His people in a special way or bring needed direction to people's lives. The leader of the meeting must cultivate a sensitivity to the Spirit so that God can do what He wants to do.

This does not mean that the leader is not to plan the meeting as best he can. This does not mean that he is to just arrive and wait on God to move. A leader must take his leadership seriously and plan as he feels led of the Holy Spirit, but he must maintain a flexibility before the Lord to change plans if He so desires.

Many times as we are sensitive to the Holy Spirit, God will move the meeting in an unexpected way. These can be some of the richest times of gathering together. People will get excited as they come expecting God to move. A certain amount of caution must be exercised here so that there are no abuses by immature believers. Personal prophecy should be greatly discouraged without the presence of pastoral oversight. But being cautious should never keep us from a genuine openness to the moving of the Spirit in the meetings.

D. Prayer

Prayer is another ingredient that should be included often in the homemeeting. Prayer can be incorporated in many different ways. It is appropriate to begin the meeting with prayer. Each meeting should also give people an opportunity to pray for any needs that are in the group. Then prayer needs can often turn into opportunities for the members of the group to reach out to the lives of others. The home group should pray for needs expecting God to hear and answer. What an exciting thing it is to hear a report in the next meeting how God moved in response to the prayers of the people.

Prayer can also be used in other ways in the homemeeting from time to time. There may be times when a major portion of the meeting will be spent in prayer. There may be special church-wide burdens that should be lifted by the homemeeting. Occasionally, a homemeeting or a district could even have an all night prayer meeting where many battles are fought.

E. Ministry of the Word

Reading and discussing the Word of God should be a very common occurrence in the homemeeting. The homemeeting should not be a miniature church service complete with formal preaching and teaching, although at times the Word may be shared in a rather formal way. The general pattern should be discussion and sharing together in the Word of God. Leaders need to seek to become skillful in teaching with a discussion method where everyone is drawn into the discussion.

F. Sharing

The leader of the homemeeting should make sure the atmosphere of the homemeeting is conducive to sharing among the members of the group. The people should feel free at times to share answers to prayer, special events in their lives and testimonies with the rest of the group. When the leader is personally aware of some of these things, he should encourage them privately to be prepared to share with the rest of the group.

G. Involvement of the People

One of the purposes of the homemeeting is to get everyone involved in some way. There are so many ways people can be involved. The following is only a partial listing:

INGREDIENTS OF A SUCCESSFUL HOMEMEETING

  Leading worship
  Opening in prayer
  Praying over a need in the group
  Organizing an activity
  Telephone calling
  Singing a special song
  Playing instruments
  Bringing refreshments
  Sharing a word of exhortation
  Giving testimonies

When people are involved in what is taking place they have a positive attitude about it. If they come week after week and only act as observers they soon get bored. Everyone coming to the meeting must see themselves as a contributor to what is taking place. It should be the homeleader's personal goal to make sure that no one "escapes unmoved".

H. Fellowship

It is important for all of the members of the homemeeting to become better acquainted with one another. For this reason the homemeeting should close with a time of light refreshment and free fellowship. This should not be considered a secondary experience to the main meeting. This is part of what the meeting is all about. Because of this, careful thought should be given to the planning of it so that everyone is encouraged to stay. The homeleader should guard against prolonging the meeting so long that there is no time left for this fellowship or so that people feel the need of rushing home without having ample time together.

  The refreshments provided should not be skimpy, but they should not be extravagant. The ladies involved in the homemeeting could alternate in bringing cookies, cakes or other refreshments. Some have preferred to have everyone bring a little something each time. This should be seen as a quality time and not an add-on.

  All of these ingredients are essential to the effective homemeeting. The leader should seek to be creative and imaginative in their use. He should seek to involve as many people as possible. He should trust God to minister uniquely to each person.

INGREDIENTS
FOR A
SUCCESSFUL
HOME MEETING

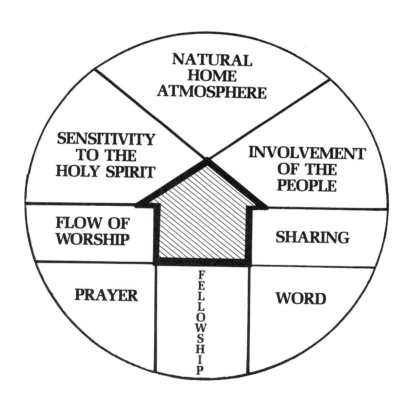

Wendell Smith

CHAPTER NINE

**Training
Homemeeting Leaders**

Every pastor wants ready made leaders. Every pastor wants mature, well-educated, loyal, gifted and submissive people added to his church on a weekly basis. Unfortunately, the people do not come in that way. New converts are likened to fish in the Bible. When fish are caught they must be cleaned and prepared before they can be utilized.

The same is true of people. If people are to be utilized, their personal lives must be cleaned up and put in order and they must be properly prepared for the task. This means that if a pastor wants good leaders, he will have to raise up and train those leaders. Putting leaders in prematurely or offering no training for them will only damage the leaders and hurt the work in the long run. Pastors must not be hasty in setting in leadership.

Training for leaders is essential if a pastor wants those leaders to perform in a desired manner. Many leaders have an honest heart, but they fail because they have not been properly instructed and trained. The pastor should make it his goal to see initial and on-going training in the lives of the homeleaders.

A. Initial Training

Initially, all of the leaders should be involved in some kind of leadership training or orientation. This training should include some or all of the following areas.

1. The Purpose of the Homemeeting

    Leaders need to be thoroughly versed in the reasons why the homemeeting is gathering so that they can constantly measure their effectiveness by those purposes. Studying this manual together would be a great way to learn together. Making this book required reading by all homeleaders would be a very good way to reinforce this training.

2. The Job Description of a Homeleader

    If the pastor is to hold leaders accountable, they must know what

TRAINING HOMEMEETING LEADERS

is expected of them in all areas. Pastors cannot assume that the newly appointed leader will automatically know what they are looking for in a leader. The job description must be clear. Chapter six of this book can be a great help in this area.

3. Areas of Character Development
   Chapter five talks about certain qualifications that all leaders must have. Certain areas could be taught on extensively, including studies on:
   - Faithfulness
   - Loyalty (see Appendix 5)
   - A Servant's Heart
   - Being An Example
   - Love and Compassion

4. Guidelines for Ministering to Personal Needs
   Homeleaders touch people's lives not only in natural realms, but in spiritual realms. As they are working in and among the people they must begin to develop a sense of confidence in ministering to some basic spiritual needs. Teaching should be included on:
   - Leading someone to Christ
   - Ministering the Baptism of the Spirit
   - Praying for the sick

5. Sharpening Basic Skills
   Many areas of ministry required of a homeleader will be quite new to the homeleader. Basic training in facing some of the various duties that he will face is essential.
   - Basic Counseling Principles
   - Christian Financial Principles
   - How to lead a homemeeting
   - How to lead worship
   - How to lead a discussion (see Appendix 6)
   - How to make hospital calls
   - How to visit people in their homes
   - How to entertain people in their home
   - How to interrelate with people
   - How to study the Bible

6. Procedures
   Every church is going to have different ways of doing things in the church itself and in the homemeeting. As homeleaders are set

HOME FELLOWSHIP MEETINGS

before the people they will be asked many questions by the people about how things operate. The homeleaders should not only understand the basic procedures and policies governing the homemeeting, they should also be well versed on the vision, procedures, and policies of the church in general. Keeping them informed will be a major aspect of their ongoing training.

All of these areas would greatly enhance the ministry of the home-leader. Prior to the establishment of the actual meetings it would be important to hold leadership training classes. If two sessions were covered each night it is conceivable that in ten to twelve weeks, the training could be accomplished. Periodically, these training sessions would have to be repeated for new leaders that come into ministry later on. Also, from time to time, further training sessions could be held for all involved in this ministry.

B. On-Going Training

It is obvious that leaders will not be fully equipped to handle everything in ten to twelve weeks of training. There is a need for on-going training and opportunity to grow. For this reason it is ideal if a monthly meeting for this purpose can take place. In Bible Temple, all of the zone leaders meet with their district pastor once a month for on-going training. These sessions would be similar to a homemeeting in structure, but the emphasis would be on training the leaders. Some of the things that would be discussed would include:

1. Discussing the need of pastoral ministry (see Appendix 7)
2. Possible homemeeting activities
3. How to handle various problems
4. Question and answer times among leaders
5. Discussion and teaching concerning various leadership principles
6. Sharing testimonies with each other of homemeeting victories
7. Updating on the vision and direction of the church
8. Encouragement and challenge

These times are also great times for fellowship, encouragement and prayer for each other in the ministry that they all have in common.

In addition to these corporate times of training the district pastor should meet regularly with each individual leader to minister to his personal needs and equip him in a more personal way. The district

TRAINING HOMEMEETING LEADERS

leader should make it a goal to meet at least once every two months this way with all of the leaders.

C. Resources

Pastors are always looking for good materials to use in the training of leaders. There are many good books and tapes available that could serve as a resource to a pastor or as a study guide to training groups. The following materials are recommended for such a purpose.

1. Books

The Making of a Leader, by Frank Damazio*
This book discusses the call, preparation, and characteristics of godly leaders. It deals with traditional concepts and how they fit into what God is saying today concerning leadership. It is a tremendous resource covering topics such as:
- True Versus Domineering Leadership
- The Heart Qualifications of Leadership
- The Balance between Gift and Character
- The Tests of Ministry Preparation
- The Law of Reproduction
- The Function of Leadership in Team Ministry
- The Leader and the Anointing of the Holy Spirit

Bible Research, by Ken Malmin*
This book is a guide to equip the student in the art of effective Bible study. It teaches through workbook assignments how to use some of the most common study books (i.e., Concordances, Bible Dictionaries, Lexicons, Atlases, etc.), how to do some of the most basic studies (i.e., Word studies, Topical studies, Place studies, Character studies) and how to organize them into a clear Bible lesson.

Team Ministry, by Dick Iverson*
This book written by the pastor of Bible Temple deals with the concept of pastoring a large church by developing a team of leaders to share the ministry burden. Practical insights and cautions are given by someone who has "been there" and is doing a very effective job.

The Christian Counselors Manual, by Jay Adams
This is one of the most biblical and sound approaches to the

HOME FELLOWSHIP MEETINGS

subject of counseling available today. Since so much of a leader's ministry involves counseling in one dimension or another, leaders must be equipped in some of the basic principles so that they can gain a confidence in this area. Jay Adams has many books available but this is perhaps the most basic and comprehensive.

*Books listed are available through Bible Temple Publications, 7545 NE Glisan Street, Portland, Oregon 97213

2. Tapes

There are many tapes on the market today on all kinds of subjects that can be used by pastors to help train leaders. Tapes should be used discriminately and should always be accompanied by a well-prepared discussion of the contents to help reinforce and possibly qualify statements made on the tape. It is important that the tapes confirm and enhance the teaching of the pastor and not raise questions in the minds of those being trained. At Bible Temple, we host the Northwest Minister's Conference annually where many training messages have been given over the years. These tapes are still available and include such topics as:

- Feeding the Flock with the Word, by Frank Damazio
- Principles of Leadership, by Les Pritchard
- Promoting Balance in the Church, by Ken Malmin
- Training a Pastoral Team, by Bill Scheidler
- The Key to Promotion, by Earl Bradley
- Practical Tips on Organization, by Bill Scheidler
- The Balanced Personality of Jesus, by Dick Benjamin
- Reproducing Leadership, by Jim Durkin
- Why Ministries Fall, by Dick Iverson
- Handling Problem Sheep, by Bill Scheidler
- Preparing Cell Meeting Leaders, by Hiroshi Nashihara
- Restoring Lost Sheep, by Ken Malmin
- Building Relationships in the Local Church, by Bill Scheidler
- Ministers Are Examples, by Dick Benjamin

All of these tapes are available by writing to Bible Temple Tapes, 7600 N.E. Glisan Street, Portland, OR 97213. All of these tapes listed would be valuable in the training and preparing of home-leaders.

CHAPTER TEN

Homemeeting Activities

The homemeeting is meant to be an on-going ministry of the church. It is not to be something that a church tries for a while and then moves on to another program. If it is going to be effective in discipling people, reaching out, raising up leaders, developing intimate relationships and equipping people for their ministry it must function on a long term basis.

This means that the homemeeting must be "alive and well on planet earth". It must be exciting. People must look forward to coming month after month and not lose their enthusiasm.

Several things will keep the homemeeting exciting. Certainly a leader who is alive and excited is a major key to an exciting meeting. But, perhaps the most important way to keep the homemeeting exciting is by having a lot of variety in the activities of the homemeeting. Homemeetings that are predictable, monotonous and repetitious usually are boring and wither away. People lose interest easily.

Since there are so many purposes for the homemeeting, there is an opportunity for a great variety of activities to take place in the homemeeting setting to accomplish these purposes. Over the long term we want to develop deeper relationships, raise up future leaders, give people opportunities for individual expression, reach out to the neighborhood, help bring people to maturity and enhance or reinforce the direction of the church leadership on a smaller scale.

All of these things will not happen each and every time the homemeeting gets together. One night the activity will focus on contributing to the fulfillment of one of these purposes. On another night the emphasis will be on another area. But as the homemeetings continue to meet and flow together all of these purposes will be ministered to.

One of the characteristics of God that He also wants to exist in His people is creativity. Creativity can be defined as "the quality of being able to produce original work and ideas". Certainly, every homeleader should pray that God will help him to develop a spirit of creativity. This is where a wife can be so helpful in assisting her husband. Much thought and prayer should be given to homemeeting activities by the leader. Last minute preparation will never produce long term, lasting results.

Creativity, however, cannot be exalted at the expense of the overall purposes for the homemeeting. Creativity must operate within bounds. Paul was willing to use various (any and all) means but the purpose was to get the gospel out (I Corinthians 9:22-23). The homeleader should use many means, but it should always be so that the intended purpose may be accomplished.

The kinds of things that can take place in the homemeeting are limitless. As homeleaders become more experienced, they will be able to share with other leaders the things that have worked well for them and, perhaps, a few things that haven't worked quite so well. It is good, however, to have some ideas to draw upon. Here are some suggestions.

A. *Sharing the Word*

The Word of God should always be a vital part of the homemeeting. It can be presented in a variety of ways but discussion is usually the best. Although most of the time the leader will have no trouble determining an area of need to discuss in the homemeeting we offer the following suggestions as guidelines.

1. Following up the specific church emphasis.

   At various times the Spirit of God brings a certain emphasis to the entire Church Body. The first suggestion, therefore, is that we use the Home Fellowship Meeting to discuss the practical application of this emphasis as it relates to the individual in the meeting. For example, if God is emphasizing the area of service, we may use the homemeeting setting to discuss how we might practically serve one another, how we might serve our leaders, how we might serve our community, etc. These discussions would certainly be punctuated by important Scriptural references relating to this area.

2. Ministering to Specific Zone Needs.

   Another important area for discussion in the various meetings is that of a Scriptural approach to the visible needs in the zone itself.

HOME FELLOWSHIP MEETINGS

Every group will have different areas of weakness. It is the leader's responsibility to spot trouble areas and bring the Word of God to bear on the situation. If there is an area of weakness, the Word of God is able to instill the necessary faith to change lives. Use the discussion time to share the Word of God pertaining to these visible areas of weakness. Using a prepared Bible Study on this area coupled with discussion would be the best way to approach the needs.

3. Exhortation and Admonition on the Christian Life.

Beyond these few suggestions, the field is wide open. We will never exhaust the Word of God. The Scriptures are full of suggestions and guidelines as to what every Christian should be. The following are some examples of what a Christian should be according to the Bible:

Abhoring that which is evil . . . . Romans 12:9
Abstaining from all appearance of evil . . . . I Thess. 5:22
Always abounding in the work of the Lord . . . . I Cor. 15:58
Approving things that are excellent . . . . Phil. 1:10
Avenging not themselves . . . . Romans 12:19
Avoiding profane and vain babblings . . . . I Tim. 6:20
Bearing one another's burdens . . . . Galatians 6:2
Bewaring of covetousness . . . . Luke 12:15
Blessing them which persecute us . . . . Romans 12:14
Bringing forth fruit unto God . . . . Romans 7:4
Careful for nothing . . . . Phil. 4:6
Careful (only) to maintain good works . . . . Titus 3:8
Casting all your care on Him . . . . I Peter 5:7
Cleaving to that which is good . . . . Romans 12:9
Clothed with humility . . . . I Peter 5:5
Content with such things as we have . . . . Hebrews 10:5
Continuing constant in prayer . . . . Romans 12:12
Crucified by the cross unto the world . . . . Gal. 6:14
Distributing to the necessity of the saints . . . . Romans 12:13
Dwelling in love and in God . . . . I John 4:16
Earnestly contending for the faith . . . . Jude 3
Edifying one another . . . . II Thess. 5:11
Endeavoring to keep the unity of the Spirit . . . . Ephesians 4:3
Enduring hardness . . . . II Tim. 2:3

HOMEMEETING ACTIVITIES

Excelling to the edifying of the Church . . . . I Cor. 14:12
Exhorting one another as the day approaches . . . . . Hebrews 10:25
Faithful stewards . . . . I Cor. 4:2
Fervent in spirit . . . . Romans 12:11
Fervently loving one another with a pure heart . . . . I Peter 1:22
Filled with the Spirit . . . . Ephesians 5:18
Following peace with all men, and holiness . . . . Hebrews 12:14
Forgiving one another . . . . Colossians 3:13
Forbearing one another in love . . . . Ephesians 4:2
Fruitful in every good work . . . . Colossians 1:10
Gentle unto all men . . . . II Tim. 2:24
Given to hospitality . . . . Romans 12:13
Giving thanks always for all things . . . . Ephesians 5:20
Giving not grudgingly, or of necessity . . . . II Cor. 9:7
Grieving not the Holy Spirit of God . . . . Ephesians 4:30
Happy in bearing reproach for Christ . . . . I Peter 4:14
Holding fast that which is good . . . . I Thess. 4:21
Holding fast the faithful word . . . . Titus 1:9
Holy in all manner of conversation . . . . I Peter 1:15
Humbling self under the mighty hand of God . . . . I Peter 5:6
Hungering and thirsting after righteousness . . . . Matthew 5:6
Increasing in the knowledge of God . . . . Colossians 1:10
Instant in season, out of season . . . . II Tim. 4:2
Joined unto the Lord . . . . I Cor. 6:17
Judging one another no more . . . . Romans 14:13
Keeping that which is committed to our trust . . . . I Tim. 6:20
Keeping yourselves unspotted from the world . . . . James 1:27
Keeping yourselves from idols . . . . I John 5:21
Keeping ourselves in the love of God . . . . Jude 21
Kind to one another, tenderhearted . . . . Ephesians 4:32
Kindly affectioned one to another . . . . Romans 12:10
Knit together in love . . . . Colossians 2:2
Laying aside all malice and all guile . . . . I Peter 2:1
Laying up for ourselves treasures in heaven . . . . Matthew 6:20
Letting no corrupt communication
    proceed out of our mouths . . . . Ephesians 4:29
Living henceforth not unto ourselves,
    but unto Him . . . . II Cor. 5:15

HOME FELLOWSHIP MEETINGS

Meek, and inheriting the earth . . . . Matthew 5:5
Merciful, and obtaining mercy . . . . Matthew 5:7
Mortifying our members which are on the earth . . . . Colossians 3:5
Not pleasing ourselves . . . . Romans 15:1
Not taking anxious thought about our life . . . . Matthew 6:25
Not fearing them which kill the body . . . . Matthew 10:28
Not wise in our own conceits . . . . Romans 12:16
Not equally yoked together with unbelievers . . . . II Cor. 6:14
Not weary in well-doing . . . . Gal. 6:9
Not sleeping, as others do . . . . I Thess. 5:6
Not self-will, not soon angry . . . . Titus 1:7
Not forsaking the assemblage of ourselves together . . . . Heb. 10:25
Not despising the chastening of the Lord . . . . Heb. 12:5
Not carried about by divers and strange doctrines . . . . . . Heb. 13:9
Not rendering evil for evil . . . . I Peter 3:9
Obedient children . . . . I Peter 1:14
Occupying till Christ comes . . . . Luke 19:13
Patient in tribulation . . . . Romans 12:12
Patient toward all men . . . . I Thess 5:14
Perfectly joined together in the same mind . . . . I Cor. 1:10
Pitiful and courteous . . . . I Pet. 3:8
Praying without ceasing . . . . I Thess. 5:17
Praying always in the spirit, for all saints . . . . Ephesians 6:18
Putting away all bitterness and wrath . . . . Ephesians 4:31
Putting on the new man . . . . Ephesians 4:24
Putting on the whole armour of God . . . . Ephesians 6:11
Putting on love above all these things . . . . Colossians 3:14
Quenching not the Spirit . . . . I Thess. 5:19
Reaching forth unto those things that are before . . . . Phil. 3:13
Ready to every good work . . . . Titus 3:1
Redeeming the time . . . . Ephesians 5:16
Refraining the tongue from evil . . . . I Peter 3:10
Rejoicing in the Lord always . . . . Phil. 4:4
Running with patience the race set before us . . . . Heb. 12:1
Searching the Scriptures . . . . John 5:39
Seeking not our own, but the welfare of others . . . . I Cor. 10:24
Separated from the world . . . . II Cor. 6:17
Serving one another by love . . . . Galatians 5:13

HOMEMEETING ACTIVITIES

Any one of these topics could be translated into a good healthy discussion by asking the group the following questions about each area of exhortation:
a. What do you think God means when He says...?
b. What are some practical ways that we can...?
c. Is there anyone who can share a positive or negative experience where they found this to be important?
d. What can we do this week to work this into our lives?
4. Creative Approaches to Discussing the Word
    a. Favorite Passage
        Ask each person to come prepared to share their favorite passage and why it is so meaningful to them.
    b. Topical Study
        Choose a topic and ask each person to contribute a scripture that teaches this topic and explain what that passage contributes to the overall understanding of that topic.
    c. Scripture Passage
        Assign a particular passage such as Philippians 3:12-16 to the homemeeting for the next time and ask them to come prepared to discuss it at the next meeting.
    d. Scripture Meditation
        Take a passage such as Psalm 46. Assign one verse to each member of the group and ask them to spend ten minutes medi-

HOME FELLOWSHIP MEETINGS

tating on it and asking God to give them special insight. Come back together in the group and go through the passage verse by verse with each person sharing their insights.

B. *Deeping Relationships*

One of the obvious purposes of the homemeeting is to help people to get to know each other better. The more people get to know one another the greater bond that develops between them and the greater the burden that they have for each other. There are many activities that can help people become better acquainted with each other.

1. Sharing Testimonies

   Giving one night to a particular family to share their life story is a good way to get to know them. Opening it up for questions at the conclusion gives people a chance to deepen their knowledge and understanding of that person.

2. Talent Night

   Have an evening where each person is to exhibit a talent that they possess whether it be singing a song, playing an instrument, making a quilt or whatever. They should tell a little about it and what their goals are in relation to it.

3. Show and Tell

   Each person is instructed to bring something to the meeting that has special meaning and value to them. They should be prepared to tell the group the story that goes with it and why it has value to them.

4. Personal Qualities

   Using carefully selected questions that every person in the circle must answer in rotation will help to familiarize people with each other. Some questions that could be asked include:
   - What is the most exciting experience of your life?
   - What do you consider to be your most valuable possession and why?
   - What is the greatest spiritual truth you have learned in the last five years?
   - What was the most life changing event in your life?
   - If you could recommend any book to be read (apart from the Bible) what would it be?

- How did you happen to come to this church?
- What are three goals that you have for your Christian life?

5. The Ungame

   Use the cards only for the Ungame and go around the room asking a different question to each person in the meeting. All questions are to be answered in order.

6. Picture Contest

   Have each person bring a baby picture to the meeting. Number all of the pictures and put them up for display. Have the members of the homemeeting guess who the baby pictures belong to. The one with the most correct answers wins.

C. Encouraging Ministry

Encouraging people to be involved, to recognize and to enter into their ministries is an important function of the homemeeting. Activities can be geared for this purpose as well.

1. How-is-it-then meeting?

   Based on I Corinthians 14:26 every one is to come to the meeting prepared to share a psalm, doctrine, tongue, revelation or interpretation. People should come prepared to share in this meeting. By putting their comments in the form of an exhortation they will have an opportunity to share and the home group will have the opportunity to be edified.

2. Family Night

   Have one of the families in the homemeeting take the entire meeting complete with worship time, special songs, exhortation, prayers and whatever else they may feel led to do. The only stipulation is that every member of the family must do something in the meeting.

3. Affirmation of Ministry

   Begin by having each person share what they feel is their ministry. After each person shares, encourage other members of the group to share positive qualities that they see in that person and how they have been a blessing in the body.

D. Reaching Out

One of the reasons for meeting in geographical locations is that people need to get a burden for their own community in an evangelistic way. The homeleader, at times, can plan activities that will fan these fires of evangelism.

1. Bring-a-Neighbor Night

   Plan a special get-to-know-you night with an activity that everyone could enjoy. A questionnaire could be handed out with basic biographical and informational questions that each person has to answer and then share with the entire group.

2. Meeting a Community Need

   Look around the neighborhood for a need that you could meet as a group. Perhaps you could find an elderly person who needs yard work done or a needy family that would appreciate a food shower. There are many possibilities here. Make it a home-meeting project to meet this need.

3. Personal Billboard

   Obtain some invitational brochures on your chuch, some appropriate tracts and spend the homemeeting night going door to door meeting people and passing out materials. Meet back at the host's home for refreshments and testimonies afterward.

4. Neighborhood Programs

   There are many government (city and district) programs that are often very conducive to bringing neighbors together. Things such as Neighborhood Watch, Community associations, political campaigning, and similar programs can serve as a base for getting to know neighbors. Getting to know neighbors on a personal level is the first step in reaching them with the gospel.

E. Social Interaction

Building relationships through social interaction is not a secondary purpose of the homemeeting. It is as important as other functions. The possibilities for activities that the home group can do together to help build relationships is only limited by the creativity of the group. Pooling ideas is a great way to plan activities.

1. Game Night

   Have each person bring their favorite table game. Divide the group into small units, serve up the refreshments, and have a good time. Group games are also good here. By dividing the

HOMEMEETING ACTIVITIES

homemeeting into teams, games like charades (acting out song titles or familiar Bible verses), Bible Trivia or group skits can be enjoyed by all.

2. Special Outings
   There are many things that people can do and places they can go that will help draw them together as a group. Not all of them can be done on the meeting night itself, but many of them can.
   - Christian Concerts
   - Hiking/swimming/Sports activities
   - Local museums and special attractions
   - Outdoor picnic and barbeque
   - Roller skating (many places have a church night)
   - Zoo trip

   It is important when planning these activities that all the members of the group are taken into consideration. Activities should be planned in which everyone can be involved in some way.

3. Eating Experiences
   Nothing brings people closer together than eating together. Jesus spent a great deal of time in eating situations with His disciples and other followers. Much variety and total involvement is the key to success here. A few suggestions include:
   - Ice cream social
   - Potluck with meeting following
   - Progressive Dinner
   - Picnic in a park

Further suggestions in all of these areas can be found in a small booklet entitled "Creative Homemeeting Ideas" available through Bible Temple Publications, 7545 N.E. Glisan Street, Portland OR 97213

CHAPTER ELEVEN

**Homemeeting
Questions and Answers**

The homemeeting can be a source of great blessing to any church. As with most programs a church begins, however, when you get involved you have a lot of questions you wish you could ask someone who has been involved with homemeetings for a longer time. By trying to anticipate these questions, we may be able to keep a few problems from arising. The following are twelve of the most frequently asked questions.

1. How Often Should the Homemeeting Meet?

How often the homemeeting meets may vary. Much will depend upon the intensity of the overall program of the church. If there are a lot of other activities taking place in the church, you may want to meet less often. If scheduling is fairly light you may want to meet as often as once a week.

Many churches have chosen to begin slowly and add more meetings as interest grew. At Bible Temple we began with one homemeeting a month and added a second homemeeting as interest for such meetings grew. It is better to have people anxious for more meetings than to have them feeling like it is too much of a good thing.

The homemeeting must be integrated with the overall program of the church in such a way that it does not compete with other all-church activities. This is why we would recommend all home groups meet on the same night and homemeetings be promoted as an all-church activity.

Bible Temple's weekly program would include a corporate Sunday morning and Sunday evening service, a Tuesday homemeeting on the first and third Tuesday of the month and a Thursday night teaching and training night. Other churches have opted for a Sunday night homemeeting replacing the Sunday night service. Still others have replaced their mid-week service with a homemeeting. Any of these models can work. The main thing is to determine the goals of your church and order your schedule in such a way as to best meet those goals.

2. How Long Should a Homemeeting Be?

When God's people get together it is very easy for them to forget all about time and to fellowship on into the night. However, because of the number of people involved, work and school schedules and the preferences of many different people, we have found it is best to have a definite starting time and a definite closing time.

This does not mean we are not open to the special moving of the Holy Spirit, but it does mean in consideration to all involved we try to operate within general guidelines. This way an occasional exception will not be seen as a negative.

Two hours is a good target to shoot for. This would be inclusive of all activities including whatever time is to be allowed for open fellowship and interaction at the close of the meeting. The home-leader should be sensitive to the time and tactfully encourage people to break up at a reasonable time sparing the host any possible inconvenience.

3. Should an Offering Be Taken at the Homemeeting?

It is a good idea to give people an opportunity to share their finances in a practical way. The homemeeting offering can be a means of reaching the needy in a very tangible way.

At Bible Temple we take an offering in every homemeeting, which goes into a separate account in the church labeled "The Saints' Relief Fund". This money is set aside for the relief of members of the church who are going through a difficult time financially. Many circumstances can arise in people's lives that involve finances and it is clear from the scripture, God's people have responsibility to the poor in their midst.

Careful guidelines should be established for the use of this fund so it will not be abused and those who have a genuine need are actually ministered to. A sample of the guidlelines we use for the fund is included as an appendix (see Appendix 8).

HOME FELLOWSHIP MEETINGS

4. What Kind of Records Should Be Maintained on the Home-meeting?

In order to give a sense of accountability to homeleaders and a record of growth and development of the homemeeting ministry, certain records should be maintained. Three are suggested:

a. The Homemeeting Report

Each homeleader should turn in a report after each meeting to his supervisor indicating attendance, offering and activity of the homemeeting. We use a triplicate form that has a copy for the homeleader, the district elder and the office file. This report is to be turned in no later than the Sunday following the actual meeting (see Appendix 9).

b. The Homemeeting Tally Sheet

A tally sheet which summarizes the individual reports should be made so the entire church program can be reviewed at a glance. The tally sheet should at least include a record of the attendance and the offering (see Appendix 10).

c. The Homemeeting Roster

Each homeleader should keep a current roster of all those in his geographical area who attend his homemeeting and all those people who go to the church but do not attend the homemeeting. This list should be constantly updated. It will serve as a reminder to the leader and could become a prayer list for the leader and his wife. The roster should include current addresses and phone numbers and should be occasionally duplicated for the other members of the homemeeting.

5. What is Recommended Dress for the Homemeetings?

Since one of the purposes of the homemeeting is to develop intimate relationships and fellowship dress should enhance this purpose. Casual attire is acceptable but careless attire is not. The leader should always keep in mind that whatever standard is set by him the people will tend to follow one step behind. Therefore, neat, clean, modest, semi-casual attire would be most appropriate for the leader.

HOMEMEETING QUESTIONS AND ANSWERS

6. How Do You Divide a Homegroup When It Becomes Too Large?

When a homegroup becomes too large, cell division must take place. Growth is a normal part of life. Unfortunately, in a group where people have become closely related any division can be seen as a negative. Therefore, church leaders must be sensitive, cautious, wise and understanding when it comes time for a division.

When the homemeeting becomes too large the leader and the district pastor should come together and discuss the situation. After plotting each family on a map, geographical lines should be drawn that will take into account several factors including the make-up of the meeting, possible host homes, the location of potential leadership, main arteries and natural boundaries in the area, and what is known about each person in the homemeeting.

From this point a leader should be selected to fill this need. If there is no leader it will be difficult to make a division. Hopefully, the present homeleader will have raised up an assistant from within the homemeeting who will be able to take one half of the group. This leader should be prepared privately for ministry.

After the leader and the home have been selected for the new meeting, the district elder should attend the homemeeting to help explain coming changes. By challenging the people concerning growth pains and change he can gracefully ease people into an acceptance of the change. Any individual problems should be handled privately, but the boundaries should be upheld if at all possible. These situations are definitely opportunities for spiritual growth in the lives of people.

When the new meeting meets the first time, the district elder should be present to encourage and support the new leadership.

7. Who Selects Homeleaders?

God's method for selecting leadership in the Bible was never a democracy. Nominations are not to be taken by the congregation followed by a vote of the people. God always used leaders to select other leaders. Therefore, it should be a function of the eldership to select and appoint homemeeting leaders. In a group of elders enough people should know the candidates so a sound decision can be made. Setting in leaders is a very serious matter and should not be taken lightly.

HOME FELLOWSHIP MEETINGS

8. How Could a Leader "Kill" a Meeting?

There are several ways in which a leader can "kill the meeting". Each leader must be aware of these things or people will lose confidence in his leadership and lose interest in the meeting. To keep each meeting alive and well, the leader should practice the following.

a. Provide positive leadership for the meeting. The leader must be bold enough to direct the meeting and to keep it from wandering off track. He must also be able to gently control group members who would seek to dominate the meeting.

b. Do not dominate the meeting. The leader must not see homemeeting as a platform for his personal ministry and dominate all that takes place. His goal should be to include others and see them released.

c. Do not use a preaching format. The leader must guard against the formal service mentality that would make the homemeeting a miniature church service.

d. Personal prophecy over each other by members of the home-meeting should not be allowed. Much havoc and harm has come from well-meaning and sincere people who presumptuously prophesied direction over others in a homemeeting setting.

e. Do not allow the same person to monopolize the attention of the homemeeting time after time. Certain people will love the special attention that a prayer time affords. If the same person constantly seeks such personal ministry, those with genuine needs will be discouraged.

5. Guard against any extremes. Such extremes as doctrinal hobby horses, dietary extremes, hypersensitivity to demon activity and others, can have a dangerous effect on people and the church. Questionable areas that are not part of the standard teaching and practice of the church should be avoided by homeleaders.

g. Do not let the homemeeting get into a rut. Be creative and try different things. People will lose interest quickly if the meeting is too predictable.

9. What is the Ministry of the Homeleader's Wife?

It is clear that the task of the homeleader is bigger than one person's ability to fulfill. For this reason, we see the leadership of the homemeeting as a husband and wife team effort. Much of the detail work and ministry to the women will be part of the contribution of the wife. In addition there are specific ways in which she will be of great benefit to the homemeeting.

a. Encouraging the women to be involved.
b. Organizing special women-related functions such as wedding and baby showers, funeral dinners, special house cleaning projects and retreats.
c. Being especially sensitive to the needs of women when they are sick, having a baby, experiencing a death in the family, etc.
d. Being an helpmeet for her husband in calling, arranging rides, organizing activities, ordering flowers and motivating others to be involved.
e. Assisting in meetings. The wife may be especially gifted in music, exhortation or other areas and should play an active part in the actual meetings.

10. What Should Be Done with Children in the Homemeeting?

Many groups that have had homemeetings have actually encouraged the children not to come. This of course takes the homemeeting out of the realm of a family activity. In reality, children can be a vital part of the homemeeting and the leader should seek to include them as much as possible when the activity lends itself to their involvement.

Children from a relatively young age are able to lead singing, play instruments, pray, read verses, offer opinions, be involved in meeting needs, serving refreshments and giving testimonies.

Occasionally because of the geographical arrangement of the homemeeting a group may end up having a large number of small children. In this case it may be best to keep the children in for a portion of the meeting and then dismiss them to another room for a planned activity with one of the adults. The various adults in the group could alternate in this function.

The important thing to remember is that children are people too. We never want them to get the idea that the things of the Lord are only for grown ups or that until they are grown up they really have nothing significant to contribute.

HOME FELLOWSHIP MEETINGS

If children are a distraction it may be pointing up a need in the parents that needs some attention. This could be an opportunity to bring greater maturity into the lives of parents.

11. How is the Homemeeting Able To Assist a Growing Church Fulfill It's Ministry?

There are many ways in which the homemeeting program can become a vehicle to assist the local church in fulfilling its ministry. The homegroup organization can be effective in the following areas.

a. New Convert Follow-up

When a new convert comes to Christ what better person to follow-up on them than a person who is in their geographical area and assigned homegroup. There is immediate contact and fellowship for that new convert.

b. Visitation

When visitors come to the church and fill out cards, they can be followed up by the district pastor and homeleader who can draw them into the church.

c. Hospital Calls

When members of the homemeeting are sick and hospitalized, the district elder and homeleader can provide encouragement through hospital visits.

d. Showers

In a large church there are always many wedding and baby showers. The homemeeting is an ideal group to sponsor these activities so that the burden may be shared by many.

e. Funeral Support

Often times when there is a death there is the need for ongoing support of a practical and spiritual nature. The homegroup can rush to the aid of the family with meals, and other practical expressions of love.

f. Prayer Chain

Every church that is organized into home groups has an automatic prayer chain. In emergency situations the whole church can be notified quickly by calling the district elders, who call the zone leaders, who call the people (see Appendix 11).

g. Organization of Volunteers

Many times volunteers are needed to set up, clean up or organize various all church activities. By rotating responsibilities through the districts the same people are not involved and called upon all the time.

h. Workdays

For churches that have workdays where volunteers are utilized for various tasks, the homemeeting can be used on a rotation basis so that the load is spread out among everyone.

These are a few suggestions as to how the homemeeting organization can be of great benefit to the overall purpose of the church. It is not difficult to see that many, many needs are met through this approach.

12. How Do You Introduce This Ministry to the Church?

Whenever a pastor attempts to bring his congregation into a new experience he must be a wise master builder going slowly and cautiously, always concerned about laying a good foundation.

The first thing that must take place is the senior pastor must be sold on the concept. If the impetus for this ministry is coming from the people or support ministries the chances for success are slim. The homemeeting ministry must be an entire church vision and the only one who can inspire that vision is the senior pastor.

The second thing which is so vital is the leadership of the church be in unity as to this ministry. There is great strength in unity. A unified leadership will be speaking one vision to the people.

The third area of importance is the foundation of teaching. People must be taught on the need for such meetings as an avenue to develop deeper relationships in the body. Teaching must be consistent over a period of time to answer all questions and develop an appetite for what is to come.

The fourth concern is that leaders must be trained prior to initiating this ministry. Perhaps a special leadership class could be held with hand picked individuals who would form the initial home-leaders. Regular times of training should take place for a significant period of time to prepare them for ministry.

When all of the groundwork is laid you are ready to follow some of the procedures listed in chapter four.

CHAPTER TWELVE

The Challenge

The homemeeting concept has potential for great blessing in any church. There are so many ways that God can use it to strengthen the church. And yet, as with any program, there are times of testing or discouragement. Pastors who feel impelled by the Spirit to introduce the homemeeting concept should realize that anything new or any departure from tradition will not go unchallenged and untested. In order to make the homemeeting a success the pastor should heed several admonitions.

1. Be Convinced of It!

The church should not initiate a homemeeting program if the leadership is not convinced that it is God's will for the church. The homemeeting will never be successful if it is treated like another "program" we will institute to bring growth to the body. It is not to be a gimmick, a temporary project, a bandaid to cover problems in the church or a pacifier to appease certain individuals in the church. It must be entered into with the feeling that the homemeeting will be the future structure of the church and its ongoing approach to the pastoral ministry. For this reason it should not be promoted as an optional program in the church, but it should be seen as an entire body function. This position will help insure the success of the homemeeting concept in the testing time.

2. Go Slow!

The leaders of the church should not get in a hurry to see the homemeeting concept in "full swing". Instead, they should be patient with people for whom any change from the traditional mode is difficult. They should not neglect to water the soil and gracefully work with those who are having a difficult time with the concept. There will be those who have been in church for a long time, who will refuse to relate to a district elder as "their pastor". There will be

THE CHALLENGE

those who feel like the young homeleader represents a "babe" instructing the mature. Do not be discouraged by this. It is normal. Time will gradually help people forget the old ways and before long its memory will fade. Soon people will accept the concept as it if it the way "we have always done it".

3. Teach Line upon Line!

Working the soil is so important before planting the seed. As leaders introduce the homemeeting concept they should build up to it with teaching over a period of time. As the water of the Word saturates the "wine skin" it becomes flexible enough to adjust to the "new wine". Teaching must be according to God's method "precept upon precept, precept upon precept, line upon line, here a little, there a little" (Isaiah 28:13).

4. Do Not Get Discouraged!

Every new program in the church goes through a cycle. It begins with a honeymoon where there is a high level of expectancy and excitement. It soon moves into a period of time where problems begin to manifest themselves either in leaders or the people. It is easy in this time of waning enthusiasm to abandon the program. But don't do it. Press through the time of discouragement. It is only as you press through that you will experience the real fruit of the program.

Every new program experiences this kind of cycle and too often leaders are tempted to abandon the program and try something else rather than work out the difficulties. For those who are committed to working out the difficulties, rewards will be great.

At Bible Temple we would never attempt to pastor again without homemeetings. The homemeeting has helped us to maintain the family spirit of a small church. It has released eldership to function in their primary ministry. It has helped to mobilize every member of the body. It has insured the needs of people are all truly being met. It has become a great channel through which God's purpose for His church can be realized.

APPENDIX

Appendix 1

HOMEMEETING SURVEY
INFORMATION CARD

NAME _____ SPOUSE'S NAME _____

ADDRESS _____ PHONE _____

NUMBER AND AGES OF CHILDREN _____

HOW LONG HAVE YOU BEEN A MEMBER OF THE CHURCH? _____

WHAT INVOLVEMENTS DO YOU PRESENTLY HAVE IN THE CHURCH?

WOULD YOU BE OPEN TO HAVING A MEETING IN YOUR HOME?

DO ANY FAMILY MEMBERS PLAY MUSICAL INSTRUMENTS?

ARE YOU INTERESTED IN LEADING A HOMEMEETING?

BIBLE TEMPLE
HOME MEETING DISTRICTS

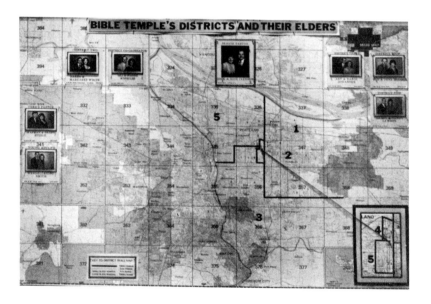

Heavy lines indicate district boundaries — light lines indicate main streets, freeways and highways. Circled numbers indicate the number of the district in which number appears.

Appendix 3

BIBLE TEMPLE
DEACON CANDIDATE EVALUATION

Name of Candidate_____Phone_____

Name of Elder _____District_____

To be considered for the following position: _____

Reasons for this appointment: _____

_____

_____

Comment briefly on the following areas:

☐ Personal Character _____

_____

☐ Marital Background _____

_____Date Married_____Ever Divorced_____

☐ Relationship to Spouse _____

_____

☐ Example of Children _____

_____

☐ Church Background _____

Date Saved _____Water Baptized _____Spirit Baptized_____

☐ Church Membership Husband _____How long?_____

Wife _____How long?_____

☐ Church Attendance _____

_____

☐ Prayer Services _____

_____

☐ Attitudes toward Church _____

_____

☐ Personal Finances and Indebtedness_____

_____

☐ Employment Background _____

_____

☐ Tithing_____

_____

☐ Personal Health Record _____

_____

☐ Family Health Record _____

_____

☐ Ability to Lead in that Capacity _____

_____

In addition to the above areas the Elder should also consider the following prior to recommendation for eldership approval:

The Elder should have:
    Visited their home
    Observed them function in this capacity
    Asked others around them how they feel about this choice

Other Comments: _____

_____

_____

_____

_____

_____

_____

I wholeheartedly endorse this candidate for the office of a deacon.

Elder's signature _____Date_____

PERSONAL INVENTORY

NAME _____SPOUSE'S NAME_____

ADDRESS _____ZIPCODE_____TELEPHONE_____

BIRTHDAY ___SPOUSE'S BIRTHDAY___ MARITAL STATUS: M M/S D W S Other___

Check appropriate boxes and fill in dates in space provided:

Accepted Christ: ☐ Husband _____ ☐ Wife _____

Baptized in Spirit: ☐ Husband _____ ☐ Wife _____

Baptized in water: ☐ Husband _____ ☐ Wife _____

Bible Temple Member:☐ Husband _____ ☐ Wife _____

LIST THE NAMES, AGES, BIRTHDAYS AND STATUS OF CHILDREN (Note the following designations under the status column: D = dedicated; S = saved; WB = water baptized; SB = Spirit baptized).

NAME	AGE	BIRTHDAY	STATUS

ANSWER THE FOLLOWING QUESTIONS ABOUT EACH FAMILY MEMBER ON A SEPARATE SHEET OF PAPER:

1. What do I feel are their most pressing physical needs?
2. What do I feel are their most pressing spiritual needs?
3. What am I doing to help meet those needs?
4. What do I feel is this person's function in the body of Christ?
5. How am I helping this person to develop into their place of service?
6. What factors are keeping this person from realizing their full potential in God?
7. In what areas of ministry are they presently involved?
8. Have they ever been ministered to by the presbytery? If so, have you read their prophecy?
9. Do they tithe regularly?
10. Do they attend the following on a regular basis: prayer service, homemeeting; action night, Sunday services?

THE DEVELOPMENT OF DISLOYALTY
By Bill Scheidler

No one wakes up one morning and suddenly finds himself disloyal. Disloyalty is an attitude that develops through various stages before it fully manifests itself. If this attitude is checked at these early stages, it may never become a problem. The importance of our sharing some of these principles of developing disloyalty is not that we suspect anyone of disloyalty, but that you can use these as a personal thermometer in checking out the attitudes of your own heart. Disloyalty sounds like a terrible word, but it progresses through some not-so-terrible-sounding stages. What are some of the stages of a developing disloyalty?

1. Philippians 2:20-21 — "For I have no man likeminded, who will naturally care for your state. For all seek their own, not the things which are Jesus Christ's."

   Many times in religious circles there is a maneuvering for recognition. This is caused by an *independent spirit*. An independent spirit is caused by a lack of brokenness and submission to the will of the oversight. An independent spirit is caused by an attitude of personal ambition. If a young leader has a strong personal ambition, he will have no love for the flock of God. He will not have a servant's heart. A minister must be first of all a servant.

2. Luke 17:7-10

   When you are ambitious in regard to your ministry it is very easy to do things with the motivation of receiving praise from men (Matthew 6:1-21). If our relationship with God is weak, we can easily shift our desires from receiving the approval of God to receiving recognition from spiritual leadership. When this is the case we have a whole crop of young ministry performing for an audience and not ministering to the people of God. They begin *promoting themselves* rather than the Gospel of Peace in order that they might receive personal recognition.

3. Luke 18:11-12

   When a man begins to think too highly of himself and his own ministry, he begins to think that his suggestions are the best suggestions. He begins to yield himself to attitudes of *spiritual pride*.

91

As a result he tries to impress the leadership with his wonderful ideas. Not only does this close him off to others around him, but it results in his own unwillingness to listen to the suggestions of others. In so doing his own creativity suffers loss. Often times a young leader cannot see with the eyes of experience a more mature ministry has. His ideas are based on an incomplete picture of the facts. Often times, therefore, his tremendous ideas must be set aside.

4. Matthew 18:22-23

   When the leadership rejects the ideas of this individual, he takes it as a personal affront. His spiritual pride has been injured. He feels that his whole ministry has been rejected and misunderstood. He begins to *speak lies* in his heart in regard to himself and others, particularly those in authority (Psalm 15:2).

5. Proverbs 25:19

   In himself he must now justify his own independent spirit. The leadership has rejected his ideas on this occasion so he feels there must be something wrong with the judgment and discernment of the leadership. His spiritual pride is at stake. He begins to use his own ideas as a criterion for the judgment of all the decisions of the oversight. As a result he develops a *critical spirit* toward spiritual leadership.

6. Galatians 6:3

   Because of the mote in his own eye, this person can no longer exercise right judgment. He begins to develop *a competitive spirit* in regard to his leaders and at times must distort facts to feed his ego. By distorting views of the leadership and contrasting them with his own views he is able to gain a measure of recognition from others around him.

7. I Samuel 22:2

   Because of his fear of failure by lack of recognition from the spiritual oversight, he begins to *gather to himself* others who are discontent and dissatisfied with the decisions of the leadership. In this way he gathers disciples unto himself who will help him feed his ego and thirst for recognition. Soon he begins to stir up discontent that becomes a challenge to spiritual leadership (Galatians 5:10).

8. Proverbs 26:27-28

He now begins to feed this group with the things that he has fed himself upon for so long. He accuses those over him of insensitivity to true spiritual authority (namely himself). He *gossips against the leadership* in progressive degrees of severity. He begins by speaking against those faults in the leadership that are obvious to all and not necessarily related to spiritual qualifications. He then moves to more obscure areas. Those around him believe him because he was right about the other things.

9. He is encouraged by the support he receives on the areas of those minor problems he has emphasized. He feels he is gaining true spiritual authority. At this point it is finally noticed by leadership, because certain things are beginning to come to *public view*. It is likely the leadership will reject him as a disloyal follower. In doing so the people who have been following him are forced to choose sides in the conflict.

10. In justifying his position, he finds it necessary to lay extreme emphasis on those minor grievances which all agree are true. People are hence encouraged to make a decision on minor issues, not really understanding the heart of the problem.

11. We now have a splinter group that begins to go its own way. It breaks off from local leadership. We have a new church that was birthed in disloyalty and rebellion. A church that begins in rebellion, ends in rebellion.

We have seen how disloyalty develops and ultimately manifests itself in separation and rejection. Disloyalty is not always easy to see externally. This is why many times disloyalty in the early stages may go unchecked. Disloyalty that goes unchecked will ultimately bring division to the work of God. It is important we as individuals use these tests on ourselves. If we judge ourselves, we will not be judged. If we catch ourselves in the early stages, we will maintain a proper balance in our character. As we work together with the people of God, let us endeavor "to keep the unity of the Spirit in the bond of peace" (Ephesians 4:3).

*NOTE: We would like to acknowledge our indebtedness to the Institute of Basic Youth Conflicts for the outline of this material.

Appendix 6

LEADING A DISCUSSION
By Bill Scheidler

DISCUSSION — A group discussion is a shared, purposive communication transaction in in which a small group of persons exchange and evaluate ideas and information in order to understand a subject or solve a problem.

A. Preparation for Discussion
1. Spend time in preparation to know the material well.
2. Spend time in prayer prior to discussion.
3. Work on an appropriate introduction to the discussion that will arouse interest.
   a. A humorous story.
   b. A testimony of personal challenge.
   c. A key scripture that will cultivate a corporate desire.
4. Make sure the room is conducive to healthy discussion.
   a. The atmosphere of the room is important.
   b. The arrangement of the room is important.

B. Discussion Guidelines
1. Get people excited about the topic by the way you introduce it.
2. Seek to involve everyone (including children).
3. Watch for those who would tend to dominate.
4. Be careful not to let the discussion wander, continually bring it back to center.
5. Listen carefully to what is said.
6. Be prepared to repeat and clarify points to the group.
7. Be aware when several people want to talk at the same time.
8. Be courteous, fair-minded and impartial.
9. Have a respect for the opinions of others.
10. Close the discussion by pulling all of the strands together so that one central thought is communicated.

C. Additional Guidelines for the Leader
1. Know the people who are involved in the disussion.
   a. Are they domineering? Do I need to back them off?

b. Are they quiet and reserved? Do I need to especially
      encourage them?
2. Be willing to remain in the background. The leaders should
   speak at the following times:
   a. To begin and guide the discussion.
   b. When asked a direct question.
   c. To clarify a muddled point.
   d. To correct an error...gracefully.
   e. To add additional information to or to summarize a point.
   f. To ask further questions.
   g. To inject humor into an otherwise dry discussion.
3. Look people in the eye when they are speaking.
4. Don't let anyone escape unmoved.
5. Be alive and alert — you are the leader. Everyone else in the
   group will catch your excitement, enthusiasm and intensity.

THE NEED FOR PASTORS

Without True Shepherds	With True Shepherds
1. Sheep are scattered Zech. 13:7; Ezek. 34:5-6	1. Sheep receive provision Psalm 23:1-2
2. Sheep wander Ezek. 34:6	2. Sheep receive direction Num. 27:15-17; Psalm 80:1
3. Sheep are lacking Jer. 23:4	3. Sheep are fruitful Jer. 23:3
4. Sheep are devoured Ezek. 34:5	4. Sheep are kept Jer. 31:10
5. Sheep are weak Matt. 9:36	5. Sheep are strengthened Ezek. 34:4,16
6. Sheep have want Psalm 23:1	6. Sheep are fed Jer. 23:4; I Pet. 5:2
7. Sheep are diseased Ezek. 34:4	7. Sheep receive healing Ezek. 34:4,16
8. Sheep are broken Ezek. 34:4	8. Sheep receive binding up Ezek. 34:4,16
9. Sheep are lost Ezek. 34:4	9. Sheep are found Ezek. 34:15; Jn. 10:16
10. Sheep are prey for enemy Ezek. 34:8	10. Sheep are safe Ezek. 34:25
11. Sheep are fearful Jer. 23:4; Psalm 23:4	11. Sheep receive rest Psalm 23:2; Ezek. 34:15
12. Sheep are despondent Jer. 23:3	12. Sheep are comforted Psalm 23:4
13. Sheep are destroyed John 10:10	13. Sheep are restored Psalm 23:3
14. Sheep are divided Acts 20:30	14. Sheep are visited Jer. 23:2
15. Sheep are robbed John 10:1-2	15. Sheep receive increase Jer. 23:3

SAINTS RELIEF FUND GUIDELINES

Because of the large number of requests that are coming to the church these days and because of the number of people making decisions in this area we offer the following guidelines:

1. *Who qualifies for relief money?*

The Bible teaches that we should do good unto all men. Individually we are to have a tender heart to all those with whom we come into contact. As a church, however, we sense a special responsibility to the household of faith (Gal. 6:10). Therefore, the saints relief fund will be specifically reserved for those who identify with this body, that is, those who are members or who are actively seeking membership (I Tim. 5:8).

2. *What questions should be asked before we release funds?*

God often uses pressure to bring forth positive changes in the lives of His people. As elders, we must be careful that we do not release the pressure before God can do His work. We must also be sensitive to help them evaluate this season in their own life.

A. Have government agencies been utilized?
  1. Food stamps
  2. Unemployment
B. Have there been consistent budgetary problems?
C. Have they been tithing?
D. What is God doing in their life? Is He trying to speak?
E. Are there any other resources available (i.e. family, property, etc.)?

3. *For what kinds of situations should funds be released?*

Almost everyone has been in tight spots in their own personal finances. Unexpected things occur on a regular basis when a washing machine breaks down or a car "gives up the ghost". These are not the kind of situations for which the relief fund is designed.

A. It is designed for emergency situations when:
  1. Basic utilities are threatened (phone not included).
  2. Food has run out.
  3. Housing is jeopardized.
  4. Transportation to work is eliminated (a bus pass may be answer).

B. It is *not* designed for such things as:
   1. Keeping everything current.
   2. Charge accounts.
   3. Car payments/repairs
   4. Clothing
   5. Etc.

4. *What guidelines should we follow?*
   In times when everyone is feeling a squeeze it is easy to lose control of our main objective. Guidelines are to help us stay on the track.
   A. It must be approved by an elder (preferably district elder). Two elders must approve any disbursement over $200.
   B. A check can be obtained from the office with the check authorization form.
   C. It should be made clear that this is a gift, but if they so desire when their situation is turned they might consider replenishing the relief fund in the form of an offering.

NOTE: Any exceptions to the above guidelines may be made *only* with the approval of three elders.

HOME MEETING REPORT FORM

Leader: _____

Describe Main Activity: _____
_____
_____
_____

Date: _____

Dist: _____

Zone: _____

Off.: _____

Att.: _____

People Absent

New Names and Addresses

Please take your copy and put remaining copies in offering or elder's box.

HOMEMEETING TALLY

DATE _____ DATE _____

DIST.	ZONE	ELDER	DEACON	OFFER	ATTEND	OFFER	ATTEND
1	1	Tom Taylor	Hilbert				
	2		Barber				
	3		Flom				
	4		Ellis				
	5		Peters				
	6		Hoiberg				
	7		Johnson				
	8		Frohmador				
	9		Pardun				
	10		Dave Chown				
	11		Bennett				
	12		Bushard				
	13		Olson				
	14		Guimont				
	15		Thoreson				
			TOTAL				
2	1	B. Brandt	Stief				
	2		Sanders				
	3		House				
	4		Derryberry				
	5		Bradshaw				
	6		Jones				
	7		Rubay				
	8		Scheidler				
	9		Maiden				
	10		Randolph				
	11		Brandt				
	12		Luckman				
			TOTAL				
3	1	Johansen	Blomdahl				
	2		Dumas				
	3						
	4		Beal				
	5		Walker				
	6		Converse				
	7		Sanger				
	8		Pinkley				
	9		Pomeroy				
	10		Nelson				
	11		Crawford				
	12		Metzenberg				
	13		Galligan				
	14		Cody				
	15		Kjargaard				
			TOTAL				

DIST.	ZONE	ELDER	DEACON	OFFER	ATTEND	OFFER	ATTEND
4	1	Isabell	Delk				
	2		Paulson				
	3		Barron				
	4		Weathers				
	5		Wager				
	6		Cruz				
	7		Sparks				
	8		Anfuso				
	9		Bennett				
	10		Chaves				
	11		Elrod				
	12		Harpham				
			TOTAL				
5	1	Lawson	Gordon				
	2		Lake				
	3		Whaley				
	4						
	5		Rock				
	6		Smith				
	7		Kaylor				
	8		Patton				
	9		Serrano				
	10		Mackin				
	11		Osborne				
			TOTAL				

101

EMERGENCY ALL CHURCH PRAYER CHAIN GUIDELINES

1. *Qualifying Situations*
A. *Life* or *Death* situation
B. Regular attender of Bible Temple or their immediate family.

2. *Approval*
Two elders must approve the situation *before* the prayer chain caller is notified.

3. *Initiation*
The emergency prayer chain is initiated by calling the official church caller. If the caller is not available, the elder initiating the chain must activate it by calling all of the district elders or their alternates (see chart below).

4. *Follow-Up*
When an answer to prayer is evident and the person is out of danger, a praise card should be filled out at the next service.

5. *Additional Guidelines*
A. Avoid starting chain within a couple hours of a main church meeting.
B. On situations that are serious, but not life or death, use the district chain or zone chain instead of "all church" chain.

DISTRICT	ELDER	PHONE	ASSISTANT	PHONE
1	TOM TAYLOR	695-2695	BOB BOWEN	
2	BARRY BRANDT	760-8604	ED MASON	
3	ART JOHANSEN	255-2078	LEIF MALMIN	
4	BOB ISABELL	256-3776	TOM SPARKS	
5	LARRY LAWSON	761-9478	DON GUNSTONE	284-5497

PUBLISHERS NOTICE

Anyone who would like to know more about Restoration "teaching guidebooks and tapes" produced by Bible Temple Publications in Portland, Oregon should write for the current catalog. Details on some of the more popular titles are given on the following pages.

Bible Temple Publications
7545 N.E. Glisan Street
Portland, Oregon 97213

Telephone (503) 253-9020

Or, contact one of our International Distributors nearest you, as listed below.

AUSTRALIA
Waverly Christian Fellowship
P.O. Box 140
Vermont, 3133
Victoria

ENGLAND
John T. Wyre
Emmanuel Christian Center
25, Southwark, Close
Lichfield Staffs
W513-75H

HAWAII
Randy Sikes
94-371C Ana Lane
Waipahu, HI 96797

NEW ZEALAND
One Way Book Centre
122 Manchester St.
Christchurch N.Z.

WESTERN EUROPE
Evangelical Bookstore
"Boekin"
Montaubanstraat 5
3701 HM Zeist
Holland

BIBLE TEMPLE PUBLICATIONS

BIBLE RESEARCH
By Ken Malmin

At last a loose leaf notebook providing individual and classroom instruction in the mechanics of Bible study. Workshops using valuable reference books, i.e. concordance, lexicon, Bible atlas, etc., are complimented by lessons on word studies, topical studies, outlining and more. A must for Biblical scholars!

THE COVENANTS
By Kevin Conner & Ken Malmin

This text provides an invaluable resource and study guide for both student and layman to use in studying the covenants. After a very important introductory chapter it is comprised of a systematic presentation of the nine Divine Covenants found in Scripture. Those who take the time to carefully study this book will be well on their way to discovering the secrets of truth hidden in "The Covenants."

THE FEASTS OF ISRAEL
By Kevin Conner

A long-awaited study of the three Feasts of the Lord in Israel, this book will be of very great value to the student, the Pastor, the Teacher and the layman alike. It unlocks some of the great truths of God's progressive dealings with His people, then and now.

THE FOUNDATIONS OF CHRISTIAN DOCTRINE
By Kevin Conner

In a decade of church growth and dynamic demonstration of the Holy Spirit's work, God's people still prize the security of a strong Bible foundation "Foundations of Christian Doctrine" provides one of the most relevant and clear presentations of the Great Doctrines of the Faith in years. The text was written to provide an intermediate approach between the more in-depth doctrinal studies and the simplistic.

HOLY SPIRIT TODAY (REVISED)
By Dick Iverson

In days in which there is an outpouring of the Spirit of God it is essential that the guidelines of the Word of God be understood and applied. Thus this textbook has been revised to better serve as a study guide and handbook on the person and work of the Holy Spirit.

INTERPRETING THE SCRIPTURES
By Kevin Conner & Ken Malmin

Major divisions among Christians today are a result of differing opinions on Biblical interpretation and application. Hermeneutics is the area in which we all might desire to rediscover the "Apostolic Keys" for interpretation. This worthy study reaches into history, methods, principles, and foundations in an effort to teach interpretation with the highest integrity.

INTERPRETING THE SYMBOLS AND TYPES
By Kevin Conner

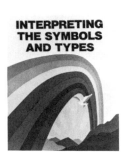

How often have we all wondered at the use of so many symbols throughout the Bible! In this book we have laid out for us, the clear interpretation of them, including a list of all the symbols in the book of Revelation and their interpretations.

LOCAL CHURCH ADMINISTRATION
By Larry Wade

A Local Church needs to function around the "5 P's": — Projection (vision), Priorities, Programs, Personnel and Precious Time. This book gives practical suggestions for dealing with these areas, and is an overview of successfully operating a Local Church as a well-administered living organism.

THE MAKING OF A LEADER
By Frank Damazio

In a day when humanism is seeping into every fiber of society sound Biblical leadership is needed now more than ever. **The Making of a Leader** examines the nature, call, qualifications, preparation, characteristics, and function of principled leadership in this day. This classic is a solid tool leaders in all walks cannot afford to be without.

MASTERBUILDER
By Dick Iverson, Dick Benjamin, Jim Durkin

This book offers key insights into building apostolic foundations for both local and outreach churches. Although authored by 3 men with broad and distinct ministries, they enjoy friendship and the mutual vision of building the Body of Christ.

NEW LIFE PRINCIPLES
By Tom Taylor

The introductory leaflet and the two manuals create an opportunity for a personal worker and a new Christian to cover together eight areas of teaching. Detailed instructions enable any Christian to be the personal worker. Fill-in lessons enable the new Christian to search out the answers in God's Word.

    —After Becoming a Christian, What's Next?
    —Personal Worker's Manual
    —New Christian's Manual

THE NEW TESTAMENT CHURCH AND ITS MINISTRIES
By Bill Scheidler

This timely book gives us a concise Biblical description of what the local expression of Christ's church is. Among other things, we have a definition of the 5-fold ministries, body ministry, bishop and deacon, and their corresponding functions. This compendium is highly readable and excellent for classroom use.

PRESENT DAY TRUTHS
By Dick Iverson

In this publication we have the backbone of our Restoration Classics. Pastor Iverson sheds light on the church from its New Testament inception through subsequent historical periods. God is still speaking today and believers everywhere are eager to know what the present move of God is, what Biblical order and government is, and to understand God's eternal purpose with the church. This book is exceptional for vision, and perspective on church history.

RESTORING THE CHURCH
By Bill Scheidler with Dick Iverson & Kevin Conner

This workbook contains notes from a six month course used at Bible Temple and other local churches to orient new members into the church. Its twenty-five lessons cover the basic areas of understanding that each member needs in order for his relationship to the church to be most profitable.

RESTORING THE FAMILY
By Dick Iverson

Designed as a sequel to the Church Life book, this book consists of thirty-five lessons on the Family in all its forms. Subjects covered include "Concepts of the Family", "Parents and Children Relationships", "Husband and Wife Relationships" etc.

THE ROOTS OF CHARACTER
By Wendell Smith

This is a character workbook designed for classroom instruction, family use or self-study, using cassette tapes. The text, based on Matthew 5, describes how to overcome basic root problem areas such as Pride, Anger, Bitterness and Moral impurity, and how to develop strong Christian character. It is designed for notetaking and instruction-response. The album of six 90 minute cassette tapes is necessary for the study of the text.

      —Workbook
      —Tape Album

THE SONG OF THE LORD
By David Blomgren

In this last day God is restoring spiritual songs to the church. This book explores the subjects of the "Song of the Lord" and "Songs of Praise" through Scripture and also surveys their historical aspect in the early church. The book closes with practical suggestions on the functioning of spiritual songs in the local church.

THE TABERNACLE OF DAVID
By Kevin Conner

As a companion volume to *Tabernacle of Moses,* this bo reveals the hidden mystery of David's tabernacle. T author has rediscovered many truths the 17th and 18th ce tury expositors have seen in this little known subject. T special value in this text is the brief history of music. Th book is vital to understanding the powerful revelation th is exploding in churches around the world.

THE TABERNACLE OF MOSES
By Kevin Conner

The author has combined a lifetime of research and thought with his God-given ability to make the Bible come alive in writing this comprehensive volume. It is probably the most complete work on this subject in print. The pictures and diagrams are excellent.

TEAM MINISTRY
By Dick Iverson

Planting new churches and church growth takes tea ministry! Here is a time-tested treatment of great practic interest to church leaders everywhere. **Team Ministry** se forth biblical precedents for team concepts, reviews trac tional forms of church governments, and lays o guidelines for setting up teams and prayerfully maintainir those relationships. At last a biblical blueprint for succe

OUTH SHEPHERDING
Wendel Smith

sed on seven Scriptural principles, this text is designed to
ıch youth workers and college students a philosophy that
ılds the lives of our young. Beyond the typical "Fun and
ımes" approach, the youth shepherd can put to work the
storal call by "shepherding the young of the flock". This
ok is a great tool for strengthening the hands of your
uth shepherds and workers.

WORSHIP ALIVE
By Bible Temple

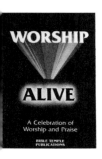

For years we have received hundreds of requests for a
music tape of our praise and worship. This is the beginning of a series of tapes of the best of the worship times at
Bible Temple. This tape is titled, **Worship Alive**, for that is
exactly what you will hear...**live worship.** May you experience the powerful presence of the Lord in Worship
Alive.

Dick Iverson
Senior Pastor

IANO PRAISE
y Mike Herron

For years we have had requests for a piano music
tape by "Mr. Music" — Mike Herron. At last he
is offering a piano stereo dream sound with
Dolby and Digital reproduction.

• PRAISE MELODIES   • DRAMATIC SONGS
DON'T MISS THIS PIANO TREAT!

WRITE FOR **FREE** RESTORATION
CATALOG OF CASSETTES, BOOKS,
AND TEACHING SEMINARS.